TRADIVOX
VOLUME IV

TRADIVOX

CATHOLIC CATECHISM INDEX

VOLUME IV

James Butler
Synod of Maynooth

Edited by
Aaron Seng

SOPHIA INSTITUTE PRESS
MANCHESTER, NEW HAMPSHIRE

Sophia Institute Press
Box 5284, Manchester, NH 03108
1-800-888-9344

www.SophiaInstitute.com

Sophia Institute Press® is a registered trademark of Sophia Institute.

ISBN 978-1-64413-356-9
LCCN 2021937574
First printing

The Manner of Execution at Tyburn.

Dedicated with love and deepest respect
to all the English Martyrs and Confessors.
Orate pro nobis.

CONTENTS

ACKNOWLEDGEMENTS

THE publication of this series is due primarily to the generosity of countless volunteers and donors from several countries. Special thanks are owed to Mr. and Mrs. Phil Seng, Mr. and Mrs. Michael Over, Mr. and Mrs. Jim McElwee, Mr. and Mrs. John Brouillette, as well the visionary priests and faithful of St. Stanislaus Bishop and Martyr parish in South Bend, Indiana, and St. Patrick's Oratory in Green Bay, Wisconsin. May God richly reward their commitment to handing on the Catholic faith.

FOREWORD

The Catholic faith remains always the same throughout the centuries and millennia until the coming of our Lord at the end of the time, likewise "Jesus Christ is the same yesterday, today and forever" (Heb 13:8). The Catholic faith is "the faith, which was once delivered unto the saints" (Jude 1:3). The Magisterium of the Church teaches us solemnly the same truth in the following words of the First Vatican Council: "The doctrine of the faith which God has revealed, is put forward not as some philosophical discovery capable of being perfected by human intelligence, but as a divine deposit committed to the spouse of Christ to be faithfully protected and infallibly promulgated. Hence, too, that meaning of the sacred dogmas is ever to be maintained, which has once been declared by holy mother Church, and there must never be any abandonment of this sense under the pretext or in the name of a more profound understanding. May understanding, knowledge and wisdom increase as ages and centuries roll along, and greatly and vigorously flourish, in each and all, in the individual and the whole Church: but this only in its own proper kind, that is to say, in the same doctrine, the same sense, and the same understanding (cf. *Vincentius Lerinensis, Commonitorium*, 28)."[1]

An authentically Catholic catechism has the function of learning and teaching the unchanging Catholic faith throughout all generations. The Roman Pontiffs indeed, taught: "There is nothing more effective than catechetical instruction to spread the glory of God and to secure the salvation of souls."[2] Saint Pius X said, that "the great loss of souls is due to ignorance

---

[1] Vatican I, Dogmatic Constitution *Dei Filius de fide catholica*, Ch. 4
[2] Pope Benedict XIV, Apostolic Constitution *Etsi minime*, n. 13

of divine things."[3] Therefore, the traditional catechisms have enduring value in our own day and age, which is marked by an enormous doctrinal confusion, which reigns in the life of the Church in the past six decades, and which reaches its peak in our days.

I welcome and bless the great project of the "Tradivox" in cataloguing and preserving the hundreds of long-lost Catholic catechisms issued with episcopal approval over the last millennium. This project will convincingly show the essentially unchanging nature of the apostolic doctrine across time and space, and so I invite the faithful of the entire world to support this historic effort, as we seek to restore the perennial catechism of the Church. The project of a catechism restoration on behalf of "Tradivox" will surely be of great benefit not only to many confused and disoriented Catholic faithful, but also to all people who are sincerely seeking the ultimate and authentic truth about God and man, which one can find only in the Catholic and apostolic faith, and which is the only religion and faith willed by God and to which God calls all men.

+Athanasius Schneider, O.R.C.,
Titular Bishop of Celerina
Auxiliary Bishop of the Archdiocese of Saint Mary in Astana

---

[3] Cf. Pope St. Pius X, Encyclical *Acerbo nimis*, n. 27

PREFACE

S OME are surprised to find that when a given Catholic is asked to "look something up in the catechism," he may well respond: "Which one?" The history of the Catholic Church across the last millennium is in fact filled with the publication of numerous catechisms, issued in every major language on earth; and for centuries, these concise "guidebooks" to Catholic doctrine have served countless men and women seeking a clear and concise presentation of that faith forever entrusted by Jesus Christ to his one, holy, Catholic, and apostolic Church.

Taken together, the many catechisms issued with episcopal approval can offer a kind of "window" on to the universal ordinary magisterium—a glimpse of those truths which have been held and taught in the Church *everywhere, always, and by all.* For, as St. Paul reminds us, the tenets of this Faith do not change from age to age: "Jesus Christ yesterday and today and the same for ever. Be not led away with various and strange doctrines" (Heb 13:8-9).

The catechisms included in our *Tradivox Catholic Catechism Index* are selected for their orthodoxy and historical significance, in the interest of demonstrating to contemporary readers the remarkable continuity of Catholic doctrine across time and space. Long regarded as reliable summaries of Church teaching on matters of faith and morals, we are proud to reproduce these works of centuries past, composed and endorsed by countless priests, bishops, and popes devoted to "giving voice to tradition."

IN THIS VOLUME

The present volume turns to the Emerald Isle in reclaiming three cate-chisms that stand together as possibly the most influential works of reli-gious instruction ever to originate from Irish soil.

As may be said for so many nations with proud ages of Catholic heri-tage, the bishops of Ireland promulgated innumerable editions of local and regional catechisms over the centuries, especially following the inspiring witness of the great bishop Richard Challoner in neighboring England, who did so much for the preservation of the faith. Toward the end of Challoner's episcopal ministry and nearly simultaneous to his publication of the popular *Abridgment of Christian Doctrine* (contained in Volume III of this series), Archbishop James Butler II of Cashel published a catechism of his own, which would become the single most influential Irish work of its kind. Although by no means the earliest catechism of Celtic extraction, it seems that no original editions of the text have survived. It is commonly believed to have been first published in 1775 under a different title, and what appears to be the earliest extant copy is a 1784 edition in Gaelic, printed by J. Boyce as *Suim Athgar an Teagasg Criosduighe*. It was not until after Butler's death in 1791 and the Catholic Relief Act of 1793 that his catechism would appear on the national stage as *The Most Reverend Doctor James Butler's Catechism; Revised, Enlarged, Approved, and Recommended by the Four R[oman] C[atholic] Archbishops of Ireland as a General Catechism for the Kingdom*, c. 1800.

Like so many Catholic works of that time, Butler's catechism was at first widely printed and disseminated as contraband: hidden in homes and used by priests and devout parents even under the most oppressive of the penal laws, which remained long in force throughout the country. In addition to incentivizing the apostasy or capture of Catholic clergy, govern-ment rewards were also available to informants for "discovering a Popish schoolmaster" until as late as 1878, with even lay catechists forbidden to give instruction in Catholic doctrine "upon pain of twenty pounds [about $4,000 at that time], and also being committed to prison, without bail or mainprize, for the space of three months for every such offense." The need for supernatural support in such trying times is made clear in Question 342 of Butler's catechism, which highlights the importance of the sacramental grace of confirmation "especially in these evil days, when faith and morals are exposed to so many and such violent temptations."

Given so many years of religious persecution in Ireland, it may be taken as a credit to the doctrinal integrity of this particular catechism that it survived the controversy of its own authorship. For, being the son of an aristocratic family, Butler was not infrequently accosted for his ingrained sense of loyalty to the British Crown; a sensibility that was not generally shared among the faithful at the time, and which might be detected in his catechism's treatment of the fourth commandment:

Is it sinful to resist the established authorities?

Yes; St. Paul says: "Let every soul be subject to higher powers: for there is no power but from God, and those that are, are ordained of God. Therefore he that resisteth the power, resisteth the ordinance of God, and they that resist, purchase to themselves damnation."

Certainly nothing objectionable may be found here, as this is simply the traditional doctrine of obedience to lawful superiors. However, given its historical context, there is a rather conspicuous silence on the corresponding doctrine of legitimate resistance to unjust laws—something that other catechisms of the period often included, typically citing the apostolic declamation: "We must obey God rather than men." It is noteworthy that the subsequent Maynooth catechisms, although drawing heavily on Butler's original text, omit its mention of it being "sinful" to resist the established authorities.

Despite the practical difficulties of its setting, Butler's catechism was vastly popular, and went on to be published in more editions than could be accurately numbered. Generations of use maintained it in high regard among Irish clerics and lay immigrants to Australia, the United States, and Canada. D&J Sadlier & Co. later published the edition restored here (New York, c. 1849), which was in turn adopted with a few added prayers as the only authorized English catechism by the First Council of Quebec

(1851), and the only approved catechism for the Archdiocese of Toronto in 1871, both of whose approbations we have retained, given the identity of the doctrinal content in these several editions. Because it was also widely used in Catholic schools of the United States, the Third Plenary Council of Baltimore considered Butler's text as a model for an American catechism in 1884, although it ultimately chose that of St. Robert Bellarmine in composing the well-known "Baltimore Catechism." Even so, significant portions of Butler's rhythmic text can be recognized in the pages of many later American catechisms.

Butler's catechism continued in print for nearly two centuries on several continents, being a clear and simple introduction to Catholic doctrine suitable for both children and adult neophytes alike. Many an Irish lad and lass have learned the saving truths of faith from its pages, reciting its answers in the schoolroom or by the hearthside, and we are proud to reclaim this classic text for future generations to cherish.

The other two catechism included in this volume are variants of a single work: *The Catechism Ordered by the National Synod of Maynooth*. Subsequent to Pope Gregory XVI's encyclical *Probe Nostis* of 1840, with its call for greater attention to the propagation of the faith, more importance began to be placed upon effective teaching methods in Catholic schools. Many religious orders and apostolates began adapting some of the more proven Catholic catechisms of history, repurposing them with various stylistic changes, illustrations, teaching aids, and content gradations for use in formal education settings. Following Ireland's first Synod of Maynooth (1875), Butler's catechism was retooled and given several additions along these lines, being adopted "by the Cardinal, the Archbishops, and the Bishops of Ireland, for General Use throughout the Irish Church," and soon becoming known as the "Maynooth Catechism," although not technically decreed by or composed during the synod itself. It is generally held as having been first issued in 1882, although the earliest copies are either undated or marked with the publishing year of 1884. That text is followed here by *The Short Catechism Extracted from the Catechism Ordered by the National Synod of Maynooth* (1891), which is simply an abbreviated version of the former, printed almost a decade later as a "take-home book" for children preparing to receive their early sacraments. We have retained its original Appendix, which contains a Marian litany and several lovely hymns for classroom use, testifying to that fondness for the Mother of God that has so long typified Irish Catholics. Both of the Maynooth texts reclaimed here are the original Dublin imprints of M. H. Gill and Son.

Given its principal use in Irish Catholic schools, the Maynooth catechism was almost exclusively printed in the recognizable Kelly-green cover that lent it the affectionate sobriquet: "the green book." Several charming illustrations were included as well, which we have cleaned and restored. It is also worth noting that the Maynooth catechism was made somewhat famous in the secular sphere by author James Joyce, who refers to it in several of his writings. Against the error of secular humanists and "freethinkers" like Joyce, first emerging in the nineteenth century and now so familiar in our own time, the Maynooth catechism continues to echo an apostolic answer to the question of whether "being a good person" is itself sufficient for eternal salvation:

> **Will strict honesty towards everyone, and moral good works, ensure salvation, whatever religion one professes?**
> Strict honesty and moral good works will not ensure salvation unless they be enlivened by "faith that worketh by charity." ... Our good works must be enlivened by faith, because the scripture says: "Without faith it is impossible to please God," and "he that believeth not shall be condemned."

All those who still seek to know and exercise the faith that is pleasing to God will draw benefit from these three classic catechisms, testimonies to the perennial Catholic doctrine and true gems of old Ireland's crown. As Butler's original still reminds readers in Question 445, the Church herself "delivers to us the sense of scripture and tradition" both by the living ministry of her bishops, and "by the approved good books, especially the catechisms, which she puts into our hands."

EDITORIAL NOTE

Our *Catholic Catechism Index* series generally retains only the doctrinal content of those catechisms it seeks to reproduce, as well as that front matter most essential to establishing the credibility of each work as an authentic expression of the Church's common doctrine, e.g., any episcopal endorsement, *nihil obstat*, or *imprimatur*. However, it should be noted that especially prior to the eighteenth century, a number of catechisms were so immediately and universally received as reliably orthodox texts (often simply by the reputation of the author or publisher), that they received no such "official" approval; or if they did, it was often years later and in subsequent editions. We therefore include both the original printing date in our Table of Contents, and further edition information in the Preface above.

Our primary goal has been to bring these historical texts back into publication in readable English copy. Due to the wide range of time periods, cultures, and unique author styles represented in this series, we have made a number of editorial adjustments to allow for a less fatiguing read, more rapid cross-reference throughout the series, and greater research potential for the future. While not affecting the original content, these adjustments have included adopting a cleaner typesetting and simpler standard for capitalization and annotation, as well as remedying certain anachronisms in spelling or grammar.

At the same time, in deepest respect for the venerable age and subject matter of these works, we have been at pains to adhere as closely as possible to the original text: retaining archaisms such as "doth" and "hallowed," and avoiding any alterations that might affect the doctrinal content or authorial voice. We have painstakingly restored original artwork wherever possible, and where the rare explanatory note has been deemed necessary, it is not made in the text itself, but only in a marginal note. In some cases, our editorial refusal to "modernize" the content of these classical works may require a higher degree of attention from today's reader, who we trust will be richly rewarded by the effort.

We pray that our work continues to yield highly readable, faithful reproductions of these time-honored monuments to Catholic religious

instruction: catechisms once penned, promulgated, and praised by bishops across the globe. May these texts that once served to guide and shape the faith and lives of millions now do so again; and may the scholars and saints once involved in their first publication now intercede for all who take them up anew. *Tolle lege!*

Sincerely in Christ,
Aaron Seng

Woodcut depicting an early method used in the production of Catholic catechisms, circa 1568.

TRADIVOX

VOLUME IV

THE

MOST REVEREND DOCTOR JAMES BUTLER'S

CATECHISM,

REVISED, ENLARGED, IMPROVED, AND RECOMMENDED

BY THE FOUR

R. C. ARCHBISHOPS OF IRELAND,

AS A

GENERAL CATECHISM.

TO WHICH IS ADDED

THE SCRIPTURAL CATECHISM,

BY THE Rt. REV. DR. MILNER.

Suffer the little children to come to me, and forbid them not, for of such is the kingdom of God.—*Mark* x. 14.
This is eternal life : That they know thee the only true God, and Jesus Christ, whom thou hast sent.—*John* xvii. 3.

NEW-YORK:
PUBLISHED BY D. & J. SADLIER & Co.
164 WILLIAM STREET,
BOSTON:—128 FEDERAL STREET
MONTREAL, C. E:
Cor. of St. Francis Xavier and Notre-Dame Streets.

Original Title Page

THE

MOST REVEREND DOCTOR JAMES BUTLER'S

Catechism,

REVISED, ENLARGED, IMPROVED, AND RECOMMENDED

BY THE FOUR

R. C. ARCHBISIOPS OF IRELAND,

AS A

GENERAL CATECHISM.

TO WHICH IS ADDED

THE SCRIPTURAL CATECHISM,

BY THE RT. REV DR. MILNER.

Suffer the little children to come to me, and forbid them not, for of such
is the kingdom of God. —*Mark* x.14.
This is eternal life: That they know thee the only true God,
and Jesus Christ, whom thou hast sent.—*John* xvii. 3.

NEW–YORK:
PUBLISHED BY D. & J. SADLIER & Co.
164 WILLIAM STREET,
BOSTON:—128 FEDERAL STREET
MONTREAL, C. E:
Cor. of St Francis Xavier and Notre Dame Streets.

𝔄𝔭𝔭𝔯𝔬𝔟𝔞𝔱𝔦𝔬𝔫

EX DECRTEO OCTAVO PRIMI CONCILII
QUEBECENSIS DE CATECHISMO.

... Catechismus vero auctore, Butler anglico sermone exoratus, utpote ab Hibernim episcopis approbatus, et jamdudum in nostra regione valgatissimus, pro omnibus Christi fidelibus anglice loquentibus, usu servetur.

In conformity with the above decree of the First Council of Quebec, we have directed the present edition of *Butler's Catechism* to be published, and do hereby declare it to be the only one authorized for the use of the faithful speaking the English language throughout the Ecclesiastical Province of Quebec from 1st October next.

+ P. F. Archbishop of Quebec
Quebec, 23rd December,
AD 1852

Approbation

FROM THE VIII DECREE OF THE 1ST COUNCIL OF QUEBEC
CONCERNING THE CATECHISM.

"Let Butler's English Catechism, approved by the bishops of Ireland and long in use in this country, be the only one taught to the faithful speaking the English language."

In conformity with the above, we hereby declare the present edition of *Butler's Catechism* with texts of holy scripture to prove the various answers, and other additions by a priest of our diocese, exclusively published by James A. Sadlier, Montreal, to be the only one authorized in the Archdiocese of Toronto.

+John Joseph Lynch,
Archbishop of Toronto
Toronto, 7th July, 1871

Introductory Prayers

In the name of the Father, and of the Son,
and of the Holy Ghost. Amen.

The Our Father

Our Father, who art in heaven, hallowed be thy name: thy kingdom come; thy will be done on earth, as it is in heaven. Give us this day our daily bread; and forgive us our trespasses, as we forgive those who trespass against us; and lead us not into temptation, but deliver us from evil. Amen.

The Angelical Salutation

Hail Mary, full of grace, the Lord is with thee; blessed art thou amongst women, and blessed is the fruit of thy womb, Jesus. Holy Mary, Mother of God, pray for us sinners, now and at the hour of our death. Amen.

The Apostles' Creed

I believe in God, the Father Almighty, Creator of heaven and earth; and in Jesus Christ his only Son, our Lord; who was conceived by the Holy Ghost, born of the Virgin Mary, suffered under Pontius Pilate, was crucified, dead, and buried; he descended into hell; the third day he arose again from the dead, he ascended into heaven, and sitteth at the right hand of God the Father Almighty; from thence he will come to judge the living and the dead. I believe in the Holy Ghost; the holy Catholic Church; the communion of saints; the forgiveness of sins; the resurrection of the body; and life everlasting. Amen.

The Confiteor, or General Confession

I confess to Almighty God, to the Blessed Mary ever Virgin, to blessed Michael the archangel, to blessed John the Baptist, to the holy apostles Peter and Paul, and to all the saints, that I have sinned exceedingly, in thought, word, and deed, through my fault, through my fault, through my most grievous fault: therefore I beseech Blessed Mary ever Virgin, blessed Michael the archangel, blessed John the Baptist, the holy apostles Peter and Paul, and all the saints, to pray to the Lord our God for me. The Almighty God have mercy on me, and forgive me my sins, and bring me to everlasting life. Amen.

The Angelus Domini

The angel of the Lord declared unto Mary; and she conceived of the Holy Ghost. Hail Mary, full of grace; the Lord is with thee; blessed art thou amongst women; and blessed is the fruit of thy womb, Jesus. Holy Mary, Mother of God, pray for us sinners, now, and at the hour of our death. Amen.

Behold the handmaid of the Lord; be it done unto me according to thy word. Hail Mary and Holy Mary.

And the Word was made flesh; and dwelt among us. Hail Mary and Holy Mary.

V: Pray for us, O holy Mother of God.
R: That we may be made worthy of the promises of Christ.

Let us pray.
Pour forth, we beseech thee, O Lord, thy grace into our hearts; that we, to whom the incarnation of Christ, thy Son, was made known by the message of an angel, may, by his passion and cross, be brought to the glory of his resurrection, through the same Christ our Lord. Amen.

May the divine assistance always remain with us; and may the souls of the faithful departed, through the mercy of God, rest in peace. Amen.

A Prayer before Meat

Bless us, O Lord, and these thy gifts, which of thy bounty we are to receive, through Christ our Lord. Amen.

A Prayer after Meat

We give thee thanks, Almighty God, for all thy benefits, who livest and reignest forever. Amen.

May the souls of the faithful departed, through the mercy of God, rest in peace. Amen.

Acts of Contrition, Faith, Hope, and Charity

In the name of the Father, and of the Son, and of the Holy Ghost. Amen.

A Prayer before the Acts

Let us pray.
O Almighty and eternal God, grant unto us an increase of faith, hope, and charity; and that we may obtain what thou hast promised, make us to love and practice what thou commandest, through Jesus Christ our Lord. Amen.

An Act of Contrition

O my God, I am heartily sorry for having offended thee, and I detest my sins most sincerely, not only because by them I have lost all right to heaven, and have deserved the everlasting punishment of hell, but especially because they displease thee, my God, who art so deserving of all my love, for thy infinite goodness and most amiable perfections; and I firmly purpose, by thy holy grace, never more to offend thee.

An Act of Faith

O my God, I firmly believe that thou art one only God, the Creator and sovereign Lord of heaven and earth, infinitely great, and infinitely good; I firmly believe, that in thee, one only God, there are three divine Persons, really distinct, and equal in all things: the Father, and the Son, and the Holy Ghost. I firmly believe in Jesus Christ, God the Son, who became man; was conceived by the Holy Ghost and was born of the Virgin Mary; suffered and died on a cross to redeem and save us; arose the third day from the dead, and ascended into heaven; will come at the end of the world to judge mankind, and will reward the good with eternal happiness, and condemn the wicked to the everlasting pains of hell. I believe these and all other articles which the holy Roman Catholic Church proposes to our belief, because thou, my God, the infallible truth, hast revealed them; and thou hast commanded us to hear the Church which is the pillar and the ground of truth,[1] in this faith I am firmly resolved, by thy holy grace, to live and die.

An Act of Hope

O my God, who hast graciously promised every blessing, even heaven itself, through Jesus Christ, to those who keep thy commandments; relying on thy infinite power, goodness, and mercy, and on thy sacred promises, to which thou art always faithful, I confidently hope to obtain pardon of all my sins, grace to serve thee faithfully in this life, by doing the good works thou hast commanded, and which, with thy assistance, I will perform; and eternal happiness in the next, through my Lord and Savior Jesus Christ.

An Act of Charity, or of the Love of God and of Our Neighbors

O my God, I love thee with my whole heart and soul, and above all things: because thou art infinitely good and perfect, and most worthy of all my love; and for thy sake, I love my neighbor as myself. Mercifully grant, O my God, that having loved thee on earth, I may love and enjoy thee forever in heaven. Amen.

Prayer to Be Said before Mass

Let us pray.
O merciful Father, who didst so love the world, as to give up for our redemption thy beloved Son; who, in obedience to thee, and for us sinners, humbled himself even unto the death of the cross; and continues to offer himself daily, by the ministry of his priests, for the living and the dead; we humbly beseech thee, that, penetrated with a lively faith, we may always

[1] Cf. Mt 18:17; 1 Tm 3:15

assist with the utmost devotion and reverence, at the oblation of his most precious body and blood, which is made at Mass; and thereby be made partakers of the sacrifice which he consummated on Calvary.

In union with thy holy Church and its minister, and invoking the Blessed Virgin Mary, Mother of God, and all the angels and saints, we now offer the adorable Sacrifice of the Mass to thy honor and glory, to acknowledge thy infinite perfections, thy supreme dominion over all thy creatures, our entire subjection to thee, and total dependence on thy gracious providence, and in thanksgiving for all thy benefits and for the remission of our sins.

We offer it for the propagation of the Catholic faith, for our most holy father the pope, for our bishop, and for all the pastors and clergy of thy holy Church, that they may direct the faithful in the way of salvation; for all that are in high station, that we may lead quiet and holy lives; for peace and goodwill among all states and peoples, for the necessities of mankind, and particularly for the congregation here present, to obtain all blessings we stand in need of in this life, everlasting happiness in the next, and eternal rest to the faithful departed.

And as Jesus Christ so ordained when he instituted at his last supper this wonderful mystery of his power, wisdom, and goodness; we offer the Mass in grateful remembrance of all he has done and suffered for the love of us, making special commemoration of his bitter passion and death, and of his glorious resurrection and ascension into heaven. Vouchsafe, O Almighty and eternal God! (for to thee alone so great a sacrifice is due) graciously to accept it, for these and all other purposes, agreeable to thy holy will. And to render it the more pleasing, we offer it to thee through the same Jesus Christ, thy beloved Son, our Lord and Savior, our high priest and victim: and in the name of the most Holy Trinity, the Father, and the Son, and the Holy Ghost, to whom be honor, praise, and glory, forever and ever. Amen.

Prayer before Catechism

In the name of the Father, and of the Son, and of the Holy Ghost. Amen. Blessed be the holy and undivided Trinity, now and forever, Amen.

Come, O Holy Spirit! fill the hearts of thy faithful, and kindle in them the fire of thy love.

V: Send forth thy Spirit and they will be created.
R: And thou wilt renew the face of the earth.

Let us pray.
O God, who by the light of the Holy Ghost didst instruct the hearts of the faithful, give us, by this same Holy Spirit, a love and relish of what is right and just, and a constant enjoyment of his comforts, through Jesus Christ our Lord, who, with thee, in the unity of the same Holy Ghost, liveth and reigneth one God forever and ever. Amen.

Prayer after Catechism

Lord Jesus Christ, Son of the living God, we beseech thee through thy holy cross and passion, through thy death and glorious resurrection, be gracious and merciful unto us and all sinners. O Jesus! hear us; O Jesus! save us; O Jesus! have mercy upon us, and strengthen our faith, increase our hope, and make us perfect in the love of God, and of our neighbor, that in this life we may serve thee alone in true justice, and forever extol and praise thee with all the saints in heaven.

Chapter 1

LESSON 1

On God, and the Creation of the World

1. **Who made the world?**
   God.

2. **Who is God?**
   The Creator and sovereign Lord of heaven and earth, and of all things.

3. **How many gods are there?**
   There is but one God, who will reward the good and punish the wicked.

4. **Where is God?**
   God is everywhere, but he is said principally to be in heaven, where he manifests himself to the blessed.

5. **What is heaven?**
   The kingdom of God's glory, and of his angels and saints.

6. **If God be everywhere, why do we not see him?**

Because God is a pure spirit, having no body, and therefore cannot be seen by corporal eyes.

7. **Does God see us?**

He does, and continually watches over us.

8. **Does God know all things?**

Yes; "all things are naked and open to his eyes,"[2] even our most secret thoughts and actions.

9. **Will God judge our most secret thoughts and actions?**

Yes; and "every idle word that men shall speak, they shall render an account for it in the day of judgment."[3]

10. **Had God a beginning?**

No; he always was, and always will be.

11. **Can God do all things?**

Yes; "with God all things are possible,"[4] and nothing can be difficult to him.

12. **How did God make the world?**

Of nothing, and by his word only; that is, by a single act of his all-powerful will.

13. **Why did God make the world?**

For his own glory, to show his power and wisdom, and for man's use and benefit.

---

[2] Heb 4:13
[3] Mt 12:36
[4] Mt 19:26

LESSON 2

On Man, and the End of His Creation

14. **What is man?**
One of God's creatures, composed of a body and soul, and made to God's likeness.

15. **In what is man made to God's likeness?**
In his soul.

16. **In what is man's soul like to God?**
In being a spirit and immortal, and in being capable of knowing and loving God.

17. **What do you mean, when you say, the soul is immortal?**
I mean that it can never die.

18. **Why did God give us souls capable of knowing and loving him?**
That we might fulfil the end for which he made us.

19. **For what end did God make us?**
To know and serve him here on earth, and after, to see and enjoy him forever in heaven.

20. **How can we know God on earth?**
By learning the truths he has taught.

21. **Where shall we find the truths God has taught?**
They are chiefly contained in the Apostles' Creed.

LESSON 3

On the Apostles' Creed

22. **What does the Apostles' Creed contain?**

    The principal mysteries of religion, and other necessary articles.

23. **Which are the principal mysteries of religion?**

    The unity and trinity of God, the incarnation, death, and resurrection of our Savior.

24. **Why are they called principal mysteries?**

    Because most necessary to be explicitly believed; and because all other mysteries of religion are grounded on them.[5]

25. **What do you mean by mysteries of religion?**

    Revealed truths which we do not comprehend.

26. **Does God require of us to believe mysteries of religion?**

    Yes; God requires of us to pay the homage of our understanding, and to submit our will to him in all things.[6]

27. **How do we pay the homage of our understanding to God?**

    By firmly believing on God's unerring word, whatever he has revealed, be it ever so incomprehensible to us.

28. **How do we submit our will to God?**

    By cheerfully doing, in obedience to God, all things whatsoever he commands.

[5] Cf. Jn 17:3
[6] Cf. Rom 10:10

29. **What means the unity of God?**

That there is but one God; and there cannot be more gods than one.[7]

30. **Why cannot there be more gods than one?**

Because God, being supreme and sovereign Lord, cannot have an equal.

LESSON 4

On the Trinity, and Incarnation

31. **How many Persons are there in God?**

Three divine Persons, really distinct and equal in all things.[8]

32. **How do you call the three divine Persons?**

The Father, the Son, and the Holy Ghost.

33. **Is the Father God?**

Yes; the Father is God, and the first Person of the Blessed Trinity.

34. **Is the Son God?**

Yes; the Son is God, and the second Person of the Blessed Trinity.

35. **Is the Holy Ghost God?**

Yes; the Holy Ghost is God, and the third Person of the Blessed Trinity.

36. **What means the Blessed Trinity?**

One God in three divine Persons.[9]

[7] Cf. Eph 4:6
[8] Cf. 1 Jn 5:7
[9] Cf. Ibid.

37. **Are the three divine Persons, three gods?**

No; they are one only God, having but one and the same divine nature; and they are from eternity.

38. **Is any one of the three divine Persons more powerful or more wise than the other?**

No; as the three divine Persons are all but one and the same God, they must be alike in all divine perfections; therefore one cannot be more powerful or more wise than the other.

39. **Did one of the three divine Persons become man?**

Yes; God the Son, the second divine Person, became man.[10]

40. **How did God the Son become man?**

He was conceived by the Holy Ghost, and was born of the Virgin Mary.

41. **What do you mean by saying, that the Son of God was conceived by the Holy Ghost?**

I mean that he assumed human nature, that is, a body and soul like ours, by the power or operation of the Holy Ghost.

42. **Where did God the Son take a body and soul like ours?**

In the chaste womb of the Virgin Mary, and he was born man of her.

43. **How do you call God the Son, made man?**

Jesus Christ.

44. **What is the meaning of these words, *Jesus Christ?***

Jesus signifies *Savior*, and Christ signifies *the anointed*; and St. Paul says that, "in the name of Jesus every knee should bow."[11]

---

[10] Cf. Jn 1:14
[11] Phil 2:10

45. **Did Jesus Christ remain God, when he became man?**
Yes; he was always God.

46. **Was Jesus Christ always man?**
Only from the time of his conception, or incarnation.

47. **What means the incarnation?**
That God the Son, the second Person of the Blessed Trinity, was made man.[12]

48. **What do you believe Jesus Christ to be?**
True God and true man.

49. **Why did Christ become man?**
To redeem and save us.

50. **How did Christ redeem and save us?**
By his sufferings and death on the cross.

51. **Was it by his passion and death Christ also satisfied the justice of God for our sins?**
Yes; and delivered us from hell, and from the power of the devil.[13]

[12] Cf. Jn 1:14
[13] Cf. Col 2:14

Chapter 2

LESSON 5

On Our First Parents, Etc.

52. **How came we to be in the power of the devil?**
By the disobedience of our first parents, in eating the forbidden fruit.[14]

53. **Who were our first parents?**
Adam and Eve, the first man and woman.

54. **Why did God command our first parents not to eat the forbidden fruit?**
To make them sensible of his dominion over them, and of their dependence on him, and to try their obedience.

55. **Who tempted our first parents to eat the forbidden fruit?**
The devil, envying their happy state.[15]

56. **Whom do you mean by the devil?**
One of the rebellious or fallen angels, whom God cast out of heaven.

57. **What do you mean by angels?**
Pure spirits, that is, without a body, created to adore and enjoy God in heaven.

58. **Were the angels created for any other purpose?**
Yes; to assist before the throne of God, and to minister unto him; and

---

[14] Cf. Gn 2-3
[15] Cf. Gn 3

they have been often sent as messengers from God to man; and are also appointed our guardians.[16]

59. **Why were any angels cast out of heaven?**
Because through pride they rebelled against God.[17]

60. **Did God punish in any other way the angels who rebelled?**
Yes; he condemned them to hell, a place of eternal torments.

61. **Why did God make hell?**
To punish the devils or bad angels.

62. **Are any others condemned to hell, besides the devils or bad angels?**
Yes; all who die enemies to God; that is, all who die in the state of mortal sin.

63. **Can anyone come out of hell?**
No; out of hell there is no redemption.

64. **How did God reward the angels who remained faithful?**
He confirmed them forever in glory.

LESSON 6

On Original Sin, Etc.

65. **How did God punish the disobedience of our first parents?**
They were stripped of original justice and innocence; driven out of paradise; and condemned to death with their posterity.

---

[16] Cf. Apoc 7:9; Heb 1:7; Mt 4:11; 18:10
[17] Cf. Is 14:11-15

66. **Did God inflict any other punishments on our first parents?**
Yes; he deprived them of all right to heaven, and of several other blessings intended for them.

67. **What were the chief blessings intended for our first parents?**
A constant state of happiness, if they remained faithful to God.

68. **Were we condemned to the same punishments with our first parents?**
Yes; we were all made partakers of their sin and punishments: as we would be all sharers in their innocence and happiness, if they had been obedient to God.[18]

69. **How do you call the sin of our first parents?**
Original sin.

70. **What is original sin?**
The sin we inherit from our first parents; and in which we were conceived and born "children of wrath."[19]

71. **Why is it called original sin?**
Because it is transmitted to us from our first parents, and we came into the world infected with it; and because it is the origin and source of every evil and misery to us.[20]

72. **What other particular effects follow from the sin of our first parents?**
It darkened our understanding; weakened our will; and left in us a strong inclination to evil.

---

[18] Cf. Rom 5:12
[19] Eph 2:3
[20] Cf. Rom 5:12

73. **What is the reason that darkness in our understanding, weakness in our will, and a propensity to evil still remain, with many other temporal punishments, after original sin is forgiven?**

To serve as an occasion of merit to us; by resisting our corrupt inclinations, and by bearing patiently the suffering of this life.

LESSON 7

On Jesus Christ, Etc.

74. **Did Christ become man immediately after the transgression of our first parents?**

No; though he was immediately promised to them as a Redeemer.[21]

75. **How many years after the fall of our first parents did Christ become man?**

About four thousand years.

76. **How could they be saved, who lived before Christ became man?**

By the belief of a Redeemer to come; and by keeping the commandments of God.[22]

77. **On what day did Christ become man?**

On the twenty-fifth of March, the day of the annunciation, he was conceived by the Holy Ghost.

78. **Why is it called the day of the annunciation?**

Because on that day the angel Gabriel announced to the Virgin Mary: "Behold thou shalt conceive in thy womb, and shalt bring forth a son, and thou shalt call his name Jesus."[23]

---

[21] Cf. Gn 3:15
[22] Cf. 1 Cor 10:4
[23] Lk 1:31

79. **On what day was Christ born of the Virgin Mary?**
On Christmas day, in a stable at Bethlehem.

80. **How long did Christ live upon earth?**
About thirty-three years he led a most holy life of poverty and sufferings.

81. **Why did Christ live so long on earth?**
To show the way to heaven, by his instructions and example.

82. **How did Christ end his life?**
On Good Friday, he was crucified on Mount Calvary, and died nailed to a cross.

83. **Why do you call that day good, on which Christ suffered so painful and so ignominious a death?**
Because on that day, by dying on the cross, he showed the excess of his love, and purchased every blessing for us.

84. **Who condemned Christ to so cruel a death?**
Pontius Pilate, the Roman governor, at the desire of the Jews.

85. **What do you infer from the sufferings and death of Christ?**
The enormity of sin, the hatred God bears to it, and the necessity of satisfying for it.

86. **Did anything remarkable happen at the death of Christ?**
Yes; the sun was darkened, the earth trembled, and the dead arose, and appeared to many.[24]

---

[24] Cf. Mt 27:45-53

LESSON 8

On Christ's Descent into Hell, and on His Resurrection and Ascension into Heaven

87. **Where did Christ's soul go after his death?**
It descended into hell.

88. **Did Christ's soul descend into the hell of the damned?**
No; but to a place of rest called limbo.[25]

89. **Who were in limbo?**
The souls of the saints, who died before Christ.

90. **Why did Christ descend into limbo?**
Saint Peter says, "to preach to those spirits that were in prison,"[26] that is, to announce to them in person the joyful tidings of their redemption.

91. **Why did not the souls of the saints, who died before Christ, go to heaven immediately after their death?**
Because heaven was shut against them by the sin of our first parents; and could not be opened to anyone, but by the death of Christ.

92. **When did the souls of the saints, who died before Christ, go to heaven?**
When Christ ascended into heaven.

93. **Where was Christ's body when his soul was in limbo?**
In the sepulcher or grave.

---

[25] Cf. Acts 2:24, 27; Ps 15:10
[26] 1 Pt 3:19

94. **On what day did Christ rise from the dead?**
   On Easter Sunday, the third day after he was crucified, he rose in body and soul, glorious and immortal, from the dead.

95. **What does the resurrection of Christ prove?**
   That, as by dying on the cross, he showed himself a real mortal man, so by raising himself from the dead, he proved himself God.

96. **How long did Christ stay on earth after his resurrection?**
   Forty days; to show that he was truly risen from the dead, and to instruct his apostles.

97. **After Christ had remained forty days on earth, where did he go?**
   On Ascension day, he ascended from Mount Olivet, with his body and soul, into heaven.

98. **Where is Christ in heaven?**
   He sits at the right hand of God, the Father Almighty.

99. **What do you mean by saying, that Christ sits at the right hand of God?**
   I mean, that Christ, as God, is equal to his Father in all things; and as man, is in the highest place in heaven, next to God in power and glory.

100. **What did Christ promise to his apostles before he ascended into heaven?**
   That he would send the Holy Ghost, the Spirit of truth, to teach them all things, and to abide with them forever.[27]

---

[27] Cf. Jn 14:16-17

Chapter 3

LESSON 9

On the Descent of the Holy Ghost, on the New Law, and the Sign of the Cross

101. **On what day, and after what manner, did the Holy Ghost descend on the apostles?**

On Whitsunday the Holy Ghost descended in the form of tongues of fire, and sat upon every one of them.[28]

102. **What does the scripture say of those who received the Holy Ghost?**

"As they were all filled with the Holy Ghost and they began to speak in diverse tongues...the wonderful works of God."[29]

103. **Why did Christ send the Holy Ghost?**

To sanctify his Church, to comfort his apostles, and to enable them to preach his gospel, or the new law.

104. **What do you mean by the new law?**

The law which Christ established on earth.

105. **Which was the old law?**

The law given to the Jews.

106. **How do you call the followers of the new law?**

Christians.

[28] Cf. Acts 2:1-4
[29] Acts 2:4, 11

107. **How are we known to be Christians?**
By being baptized, by professing the doctrine of Christ, and by the sign of the cross.

108. **How is the sign of the cross made?**
By putting the right hand to the forehead, then under the breast, then to the left and right shoulders; saying, "In the name of the Father, and of the Son, and of the Holy Ghost. Amen."

109. **Why do you make the sign of the cross?**
To beg that Jesus Christ, by his cross and passion, may bless and protect me.

110. **Should we frequently make the sign of the cross?**
Yes; particularly in all temptations and dangers, and before and after prayer; and always with great attention and devotion.

111. **What does the sign of the cross signify?**
It signifies and brings to our minds the principal mysteries of religion.

112. **What mysteries of religion does the sign of the cross recall to our minds?**
The Blessed Trinity, and the incarnation and death of our Savior.

113. **How does the sign of the cross remind us of the Blessed Trinity?**
Because in making the sign of the cross, we invoke the three divine Persons; saying, "In the name of the Father, and of the Son, and of the Holy Ghost."

114. **How does the sign of the cross bring to our minds the incarnation and death of our Savior?**
Because as he suffered death in human flesh on a cross, the sign of the cross must naturally remind all true Christians of his incarnation and death.

115. **Where are true Christians to be found?**
In the true Church.

LESSON 10

On the True Church

116. **What do you mean by the true Church?**
The congregation of all the faithful, who, being baptized, profess the same doctrine, partake of the same sacraments, and are governed by their lawful pastors, under one visible head on earth.

117. **How do you call the true Church?**
The holy Catholic Church.

118. **Is there any other true Church, besides the holy Catholic Church?**
No; as there is but "one Lord, one faith, one baptism, one God, one Father of all,"[30] there is but one true Church.

119. **Are all obliged to be of the true Church?**
Yes; "he that believeth not shall be condemned."[31]

120. **Can persons who deny outwardly the true religion or Church, in which they inwardly believe, expect salvation while in that state?**
No. Whosoever, says Christ, "shall deny me before man, I will also deny him before my Father who is in heaven."[32]

121. **Is a person in the way of salvation who believes in the true Church and says that in his heart he is attached to it, but through pride, human respect, or worldly motives does not make open profession of it, or does not comply with its essential duties?**
No; St. Paul says, "With the heart we believe unto justice; but with the mouth confession is made unto salvation."[33]

---

[30] Eph 4:5-6
[31] Mk 16:16; Cf. Acts 2:47; Lk 10:15; Jn 10:16; Mt 18:17
[32] Mt 10:33
[33] Rom 10:10

122. **Will strict honesty to everyone and moral good works ensure salvation, whatever church or religion one professes?**

No; good words must be enlivened by "faith, that worketh by charity."[34]

123. **Why must our good works be enlivened by faith?**

Because the scriptures say, "without faith it is impossible to please God."[35]

124. **Are we justified by faith alone, without good works?**

No; "As the body without the spirit is dead, so also faith without works is dead."[36]

125. **Must our good works be also enlivened by charity?**

Yes; for St. Paul says: "If I should deliver all my goods to feed the poor, and if I should deliver my body to be burned, and have not charity, it profiteth me nothing."[37]

126. **What is that charity of which St. Paul speaks?**

That pure and sincere love for God, which makes us do his will in all things; and be obedient to his Church, which he commands us to hear.[38]

127. **Which are the marks and signs of the true Church?**

The true Church is one, holy, Catholic, and apostolical.

128. **How is the Church one?**

In being one body and one fold, animated by one spirit, under one head, and one shepherd, Jesus Christ, who is over all the Church.[39]

[34] Gal 5:6
[35] Heb 11:6
[36] Jas 2:26
[37] 1 Cor 13:3
[38] Cf. Mt 18:17; Lk 10:16
[39] Cf. Eph 4:4

129. **In what else is the Church one?**

In all its members believing the same truths, having the same sacraments and sacrifice, and being under one visible head on earth.

130. **How is the Church holy?**

In its founder, Jesus Christ; in its doctrine and sacraments; and in numbers of its children, who have been eminent for holiness in all ages.

131. **How is the Church catholic or universal?**

Because it has subsisted in every age, and is to last to the end of time, and is spread throughout all nations.[40]

132. **How is the Church apostolical?**

Because it was founded by Christ on his apostles, and was governed by them and their lawful successors; and because it never ceased, and never will cease to teach their doctrine.[41]

LESSON 11

The Church Continued

133. **Why do we call the Church Roman?**

Because the visible head of the Church is bishop of Rome; and because St. Peter and his successors fixed their see in Rome.

134. **Who is the visible head of the Church?**

The pope: who is Christ's vicar on earth, and supreme visible head of the Church.

---

[40] Cf. Mt 28:18-20
[41] Cf. Eph 2:20; Mt 28:20

135. **To whom does the pope succeed, as visible head of the Church?**
To St. Peter, who was the chief of the apostles, Christ's vicar on earth, and first pope and bishop of Rome.

136. **What texts of scripture prove that St. Peter was made head of the Church?**
Chiefly the words which Christ said to him: "Thou art Peter, and upon this rock I will build my church. And I will give to thee the keys of the kingdom of heaven"[42] "Feed my lambs...Feed my sheep."[43]

137. **What do these texts prove?**
That Christ committed to St. Peter and to his lawful successors, the care of his whole flock, that is, of his whole Church, both pastors and people.

138. **Who succeeds to the other apostles?**
The bishops of the holy Catholic Church.

139. **Can the Church err in what it teaches?**
No; because Christ promised to the pastors of his Church: "Behold I am with you all days, even to the consummation of the world."[44]

140. **Why did Christ promise always to remain with his Church?**
That he himself, directing and assisting by his Holy Spirit the pastors of his Church, might teach all ages and nations.

141. **What else did Christ promise to his Church?**
That "the gates of hell shall not prevail against it."[45]

142. **What other advantage have we in the true Church?**
We have true faith, with the communion of saints and the forgiveness of sins.

[42] Mt 16:18-19
[43] Jn 21:15, 16, 17
[44] Mt 28:20
[45] Mt 16:18

143. What means the forgiveness of sins?

That Christ left to the pastors of his Church the power of forgiving sins.[46]

Chapter 4

LESSON 12

On Sin

144. What is actual sin?

Any willful thought, word, deed, or omission, contrary to the law of God.

145. How many kinds of actual sin are there?

Two: mortal and venial.

146. What is mortal sin?

A grievous offense or transgression against the law of God.

147. Why is it called mortal?

Because it kills the soul, by depriving it of its true life, which is sanctifying grace—and because it brings everlasting death and damnation on the soul.

148. Does venial sin deprive the soul of sanctifying grace, and deserve everlasting punishment?

No; but it hurts the soul by lessening its love for God, and by disposing to mortal sin. The scriptures say: "He that contemneth small things, shall fall by little and little."[47]

---

[46] Cf. Jn 20:23
[47] Ecclus 19:1

149. **What is sanctifying grace?**
That grace which sanctifies the soul, and makes it pleasing to God.

150. **What do you mean by grace?**
A supernatural gift, destined by God for our sanctification, and to enable us to merit heaven.

151. **Is grace necessary to salvation?**
Yes; "without me," says Christ, "you can do nothing."[48]

152. **Is it a great misfortune to fall into mortal sin?**
It is the greatest of all misfortunes.

153. **What should we do, when we have fallen into mortal sin?**
We should repent sincerely; and go to confession as soon as possible.

154. **Why should we go to confession after we have fallen into mortal sin?**
That we may recover God's friendship, and be always prepared to die.

155. **What should we do, if we cannot go to confession when we fall into mortal sin?**
We should excite ourselves to perfect contrition, with a sincere desire of going to confession as soon as we can.

156. **How do you express an act of perfect contrition?**
O my God, I am heartily sorry for having offended thee, and I detest my sins most sincerely, not only because by them I have lost all right to heaven, and have deserved the everlasting torments of hell, but especially because they displease thee, my God, who art so deserving of all my love, on account of thy infinite goodness, and most amiable perfections; and I firmly resolve, by thy holy grace, never more to offend thee, and to amend my life.

[48] Jn 15:5

157. **Will perfect contrition reconcile us to God when we cannot go to confession?**

Yes; and it is the only means we have to recover God's friendship when we cannot go to confession.

158. **What is necessary for our contrition to be perfect?**

That we should be truly sorry for our sins, because they are offensive to God, who is so good in himself; with a sincere resolution not to offend God anymore; to satisfy for our sins, and to go to confession as soon as we can.

159. **How many are the chief mortal sins, commonly called capital and deadly sins?**

Seven:
1. Pride.
2. Covetousness.
3. Lust.
4. Anger.
5. Gluttony.
6. Envy.
7. Sloth.

On the Sins against the Holy Ghost and Those That Cry for Vengeance, and the Four Last Things

160. **Which are the signs against the Holy Ghost?**[49]

These six:
1. Despair of salvation.
2. Presumption of God's mercy, without amending one's life.
3. To impugn the known truth, in matters of faith and religion.
4. Envy at another's spiritual good.

---

[49] Editor's note: Questions 160-165 were moved here from an appendix in the original.

5. Obstinacy in sin, and,

6. Final impenitence.

161. **Why are these called sins against the Holy Ghost?**

Because they directly oppose and affront the infinite goodness of God.

162. **Why does our Savior say that sins against the Holy Ghost "shall not be forgiven, neither in this world, nor in the world to come"?**[50]

Because those, who are guilty of the five first of those sins, seldom or ever do repent of such sins, and are with great difficulty brought to be sorry for them; and those that are guilty of the last, or final impenitence, never can repent; but dying in mortal guilt, and enemies to God, are incapable of forgiveness.

163. **What are the sins that cry to heaven for vengeance?**

These four:

1. Willful murder.

2. The sins of Sodom.

3. Oppression of the poor, and,

4. Defrauding laborers of their wages.

164. **What are the four last things to be remembered?**

1. Death.

2. Judgment.

3. Heaven.

4. Hell.

165. **Is the frequent remembrance of these things useful to the soul?**

It is a most powerful preservative against sin; for the scripture says, "In all thy works remember thy last end; and thou shalt never sin."[51]

---

[50] Mt 12:32
[51] Ecclus 7:40

166. **Where shall they go who die in mortal sin?**

To hell, for all eternity.

167. **Where do they go who die in venial sin?**

To purgatory.

LESSON 13

On Purgatory

168. **What is purgatory?**

A place of punishment in the other life, where some souls suffer for a time before they can go to heaven.[52]

169. **Do any others go to purgatory besides those who die in venial sin?**

Yes; all who die indebted to God's justice on account of mortal sin.

170. **When God forgives mortal sin, as to the guilt of it, and the eternal punishment it deserved, does he require temporary punishments to be suffered for it?**

Yes; very often, for our correction—to deter us from relapsing into sin; and that we should make some atonement to his offended justice and goodness.[53]

171. **Can the souls in purgatory be relieved by our prayers and other good works?**

Yes; being children of God, and still members of the Church, they share in the communion of saints; and the scripture says, "It is a holy and wholesome thought to pray for the dead, that they may be loosed from their sins."[54]

[52] Cf. Mt 12:32
[53] Cf. Nm 14:23; 2 Kgs 12-14
[54] 2 Mc 12:46

172. **What means the communion of saints?**
It means that all who belong to the true Church, by their prayers and good works assist each other.

173. **Is it sufficient for salvation to be members of the true Church?**
No; we must avoid evil and do good.[55]

174. **"What good shall I do that I may have life everlasting?"**[56]
"If thou wilt enter into life," says Christ, "keep the commandments."[57]

175. **What commandments am I to keep?**
The ten commandments of God.

Chapter 5

LESSON 14

On the Ten Commandments

176. **Say the ten commandments of God.**[58]
1. I am the Lord thy God, thou shalt not have strange gods before me, etc.
2. Thou shalt not take the name of the Lord thy God in vain.
3. Remember that thou keep holy the sabbath-day.
4. Honor thy father and thy mother.
5. Thou shalt not kill.
6. Thou shalt not commit adultery.
7. Thou shalt not steal.

[55] Cf. 1 Pt 3:11
[56] Mt 19:16
[57] Mt 19:17
[58] Cf. Ex 20 and Appendix below

8. Thou shalt not bear false witness against thy neighbor.

9. Thou shalt not covet thy neighbor's wife.

10. Thou shalt not covet thy neighbor's goods.

177. **Is it necessary to keep all and every one of the ten commandments?**
Yes; the scripture says, whosoever shall "offend in one, is become guilty of all,"[59] that is, the observance of the other commandments will not avail him to salvation.

178. **Which is the first commandment?**
I am the Lord thy God, thou shalt not have strange gods before me.

179. **What is commanded by the first commandment?**
To adore one God, and to adore but him alone.

180. **How are we to adore God?**
By faith, hope, and charity; by prayer and sacrifice.

181. **What is faith?**
A divine virtue, by which we firmly believe what God has taught.

182. **How do we know with certainty what God has taught?**
By the authority of his Church, which is "the pillar and ground of truth."[60]

183. **Why do we believe what God has taught?**
Because he is the infallible truth, and therefore cannot deceive, nor be deceived.

184. **What is hope?**
A divine virtue, by which we firmly hope for eternal life, and for the means to obtain it.

[59] Jas 2:10
[60] 1 Tm 3:15

185. **Why do we hope in God?**

Because he is infinitely powerful, good and merciful; and because he is faithful to his word, and has promised all graces, even heaven itself, through Jesus Christ, to all those who keep his commandments.

186. **What is charity?**

A divine virtue, by which we love God above all for his own sake; and our neighbors as ourselves for the love of God.

187. **Why should we love God above all for his own sake?**

Because God alone is infinitely good and perfect.

188. **How are we to love God above all?**

By loving him more than ourselves, and more than anything in the world; and by being disposed to sacrifice everything that is most dear to us, even our very lives, if necessary, rather than to offend him.

189. **Should we often make acts of faith, hope, and charity?**

Yes; and particularly when we come to the use of reason, and at the hour of death; also when we are tempted to sin, or have sinned against those divine virtues; and when we prepare ourselves to receive any sacrament.

LESSON 15

On the First Commandment

190. **What is forbidden by the first commandment?**

All sins against faith, hope, and charity, and other duties of religion.

191. **How does a person sin against faith?**

By not endeavoring to know what God has taught, by not believing all that God has taught, and by not professing his belief in what God has taught.

192. **Who are they who do not endeavor to know what God has taught?**

They who neglect to learn the Christian doctrine.

193. **Who are they who do not believe all that God has taught?**

Heretics and infidels.

194. **Who are they who sin against faith by not professing their belief in what God has taught?**

All those who by any outward act, profession, or declaration deny the true religion or Church in which they inwardly believe.

195. **When, in particular, are we obliged to make open profession of our faith or religion?**

As often as God's honor, our own spiritual good, or our neighbor's edification requires it. "Whosoever," says Christ, "shall confess me before men; I will also confess him before my Father who is in heaven."[61]

196. **What does St. Paul say of apostates, that is, of those who are fallen away from the true religion or Church?**

That it is impossible for them to be renewed again to penance;[62] that is, their conversion is extremely difficult.

197. **Why is the conversion of apostates so very difficult?**

Because, by their apostasy they crucify again the Son of God, and make a mockery of him.[63]

198. **Which are the sins against hope?**

Despair and presumption.

199. **What is despair?**

A diffidence in God's mercy.

---

[61] Mt 10:32
[62] Cf. Heb 6:4-6
[63] Cf. Heb 6:6

200. **What is presumption?**
A foolish expectation of salvation, without making proper use of the necessary means to obtain it.

201. **How does a person sin against the love of God?**
By every sin, but particularly by mortal sin.

202. **How does a person sin against the love of his neighbor?**
By injuring him in any respect; and by not assisting him, when able, in his spiritual or corporal necessities.

LESSON 16

The First Commandment Continued

203. **What else is forbidden by the first commandment?**
To give to any creature the honor due to God alone.

204. **Are we forbidden to honor the saints?**
No; if we only honor them as God's special friends and faithful servants, and if we do not give them supreme or divine honor, which belongs to God alone.

205. **How do Catholics distinguish between the honor they give to God, and the honor they give to the saints, when they pray to God and the saints?**
Of God alone they beg grace and mercy; and of the saints they only ask the assistance of their prayers.[64]

---

[64] Cf. Tb 12:12

206. Is it lawful to recommend ourselves to the saints, and to ask their prayers?

Yes; as it is lawful and a very pious practice to ask the prayers of our fellow creatures on earth, and to pray for them.[65]

207. Why do Catholics kneel before the images of Christ and of his saints?

To honor Christ and his saints, whom their images represent.[66]

208. Is it proper to show any mark of respect to the crucifix and to the pictures of Christ and his saints?

Yes; because they relate to Christ and his saints, being representations and memorials of them.[67]

209. Why do Catholics honor the relics of the saints?

Because their bodies have been the temples of the Holy Ghost, and at the last day will be honored and glorified forever in heaven.[68]

210. May we then pray to the crucifix, or to the images, or relics of the saints?

By no means; for they have neither life, nor sense, nor power to hear or help us.

211. Why then do we pray before the crucifix, and before the images and relics of the saints?

Because they enliven our devotion, by exciting pious affections and desires, and reminding us of Christ and his saints; they also encourage us to imitate their virtues and good works.[69]

212. Is it not forbidden by the first commandment to make images?

No; if we do not make them for gods, to adore and serve them, as the idolaters did.

---

[65] Cf. 1 Thes 5:25; Jas 5:16
[66] Cf. Ex 25:18-22
[67] Cf. Acts 19:12
[68] Cf. Mt 9:20-21
[69] Cf. Ex 25:18-22; Jn 3:14

213. **Is there anything else forbidden by the first commandment?**

Yes; all dealings and communications with the devil; and inquiring after things lost, hidden, or to come, by improper means.

214. **Are crediting dreams, fortune-telling, and the like superstitious practices, also forbidden?**

Yes; and all incantations, charms, and spells; also, idle observation of omens and accidents, and all such nonsensical remarks.

215. **What do you think of theatrical representations in which religion, its ministers, and sacred rites are ridiculed?**

They are impious and highly criminal, and strictly forbidden by the first commandment.

Chapter 6

LESSON 17

On the Second, Third, and Fourth Commandments

216. **Say the second commandment.**

Thou shalt not take the name of the Lord thy God in vain.

217. **What is commanded by the second commandment?**

To speak with reverence of God, of his saints and ministers, of religion, its practices and ceremonies, and of all things relating to divine service.

218. **What else is commanded by the second commandment?**

To keep our lawful oaths and vows.

219. **What is forbidden by the second commandment?**

All false, rash, unjust, and unnecessary oaths; also, cursing, swearing, blaspheming, and profane words.[70]

220. **Is it ever lawful to swear?**

It is; when God's honor, our own or our neighbor's good, or necessary defense require it.

221. **What do you mean by an unjust oath?**

An oath injurious to God, to ourselves, or to our neighbors.

222. **Is a person obliged to keep an unjust oath?**

No; he sinned in taking it, and would sin more grievously in keeping it.

223. **Is a person obliged to keep a lawful oath?**

Yes; and it would be perjury to break it.

224. **What is perjury?**

To break a lawful oath, or to take a false one.

225. **Is perjury a great sin?**

It is a most grievous sin.

226. **Say the third commandment.**

Remember that thou keep holy the sabbath-day.

227. **What is commanded by the third commandment?**

To sanctify the Sunday.

228. **Which is the chief duty by which we are commanded to sanctify the Sunday?**

Assisting at the Holy Sacrifice of the Mass.

---

[70] Cf. Mt 5:34; Jas 5:12

229. **What other religious exercises are recommended to sanctify the Sunday?**
Attending vespers, reading moral and pious books, and going to Communion.

230. **What particular good works are recommended to sanctify the Sunday?**
The works of mercy, spiritual and corporal; and particularly to instruct the ignorant in the way of salvation, by word and example.[71]

231. **What is forbidden by the third commandment?**
All unnecessary servile work; and whatever may hinder the due observance of the Lord's day, or tend to profane it.

232. **Say the fourth commandment.**
Honor thy father and thy mother.

233. **What is commanded by the fourth commandment?**
To love, honor, and obey parents and superiors.[72]

234. **What is forbidden by the fourth commandment?**
All contempt, stubbornness, ill-will, and disobedience to parents and superiors.

235. **What are the chief duties of parents?**
To provide for their children; to instruct them and all others under their care in the Christian doctrine; and by every means in their power to lead them to God.[73]

236. **What special reward has God promised to dutiful children?**
A long and happy life, even in this world.[74]

[71] Cf. Dn 12:3
[72] Cf. Col 3:20
[73] Cf. 1 Tm 5:8
[74] Cf. Eph 6:1-3

237. What are the duties of citizens towards the civil government?

To obey the laws and respect the public officers, not only for wrath, but also for conscience sake; for so is the will of God.[75] We should likewise pray "for all who are in high stations, that we may lead a quiet and peaceable life."[76]

238. Is it sinful to resist the established authorities?

Yes; St. Paul says: "Let every soul be subject to higher powers: for there is no power but from God, and those that are, are ordained of God. Therefore he that resisteth the power, resisteth the ordinance of God, and they that resist, purchase to themselves damnation."[77]

239. What are the chief duties of masters to their servants, apprentices, and all others under their care?

To lead them to God by word and example; to see that they be exact in their religious duties; to treat them with justice and humanity; and to correct and reprove them, when necessary.

240. What does St. Paul say to masters?

"Masters, do to your servants that which is just and equal; knowing that you also have a master in heaven."[78]

241. What are the chief duties of servants and apprentices to their masters?

To be obedient, respectful, and faithful to them; to be diligent in their work and services, and not to suffer their masters to be injured in their property by any person.[79]

[75] Cf. 1 Pt 2:13ff; Rom 13:1-8
[76] 1 Tm 2:2
[77] Rom 13:1-2
[78] Col 4:1
[79] Cf. Eph 6:5-8; Col 3:22-24

LESSON 18

On the Fifth, Sixth, Seventh, and Eighth Commandments

242. **Say the fifth commandment?**

Thou shalt not kill.

243. **What is forbidden by the fifth commandment?**

All willful murder, quarrelling, fighting, hatred, anger, and revenge.

244. **What else is forbidden by the fifth commandment?**

All injurious words; giving scandal or bad example; and not to ask pardon of those whom we have offended.[80]

245. **Say the sixth commandment.**

Thou shalt not commit adultery.

246. **What is forbidden by the sixth commandment?**

All unchaste freedoms with another's wife or husband.

247. **What else is forbidden by the sixth commandment?**

All immodest looks, words, or actions; and everything that is contrary to chastity.[81]

248. **Are immodest songs, discourses, plays, novels, and comedies forbidden by the sixth commandment?**

Yes; and it is sinful to join in them, to encourage them, or to be present at them.

249. **Say the seventh commandment.**

Thou shalt not steal.

---

[80] Cf. Mt 5:39
[81] Cf. Col 3:5-6

250. **What is forbidden by the seventh commandment?**

All unjust taking or keeping what belongs to another.

251. **What else is forbidden by the seventh commandment?**

All cheating in buying or selling; or any other injury done our neighbor in his property.[82]

252. **What is commanded by the seventh commandment?**

To pay our lawful debts; and to give everyone his own.

253. **What are they obliged to do, who retain ill-got goods, or who have unjustly what belongs to another?**

To restore them as soon as possible, and as far as they are able; otherwise the sin will not be forgiven them.

254. **Say the eighth commandment.**

Thou shalt not bear false witness against thy neighbor.

255. **What is forbidden by the eighth commandment?**

All false testimonies, rash judgments, and lies.[83]

256. **Is it lawful to tell an innocent or jocose lie, or to tell a lie for a good purpose?**

No lie can be lawful or innocent; and no motive, however good, can excuse a lie; because a lie is always sinful and bad in itself.[84]

257. **What else is forbidden by the eighth commandment?**

Backbiting, calumny, and detraction; and all words and speeches hurtful to our neighbor's honor or reputation.

---

[82] Cf. 1 Cor 6:10
[83] Cf. Mt 7:1
[84] Cf. Jn 8:44

258. **What is commanded by the eighth commandment?**
To speak of others with justice and charity, as we would be glad they did speak of us; and to witness the truth in all things.

259. **What must they do who have given false evidence against a neighbor, or who have spoken ill of him, or injured his character in any respect?**
They must repair the injury done him, as far as they are able; and make him satisfaction by restoring his good name as soon as possible: otherwise the sin will not be forgiven them.

LESSON 19

On the Ninth and Tenth Commandments

260. **Say the ninth commandment.**
Thou shalt not covet thy neighbor's wife.

261. **What is forbidden by the ninth commandment?**
All immodest thoughts and desires, and willful pleasures in them.

262. **What else is forbidden by the ninth commandment?**
All immediate occasions of immodest thoughts and desires.

263. **What are the immediate occasions of immodest thoughts and desires?**
Unchaste words and discourses; immodest books and pictures; and all amusements dangerous to chastity.

264. **What else may be deemed immediate occasions of immodest thoughts and desires?**
Lascivious looks and touches; idleness; bad company; all excess in eating and drinking; and whatever tends to inflame the passions.

265. **Is it sinful to have unchaste thoughts, when there is no desire or intention to indulge them, by any criminal action?**

They are always very dangerous, and when entertained deliberately and with pleasure, they defile the soul like criminal actions.[85]

266. **Say the tenth commandment.**

Thou shalt not covet thy neighbor's goods.

267. **What is forbidden by the tenth commandment?**

All covetous thoughts and unjust desire of our neighbor's goods or profit.

268. **To how many commandments may the ten commandments be reduced?**

To these two principal commandments: "Thou shalt love the Lord thy God, with thy whole heart, and with thy whole soul, and with all thy strength, and with all thy mind, and thy neighbor as thyself...this do and thou shalt live."[86]

269. **"And who is my neighbor?"[87]**

Mankind of every description, and without any exception of persons, even those who injure us, or differ from us in religion.

270. **How am I to love my neighbor as myself?**

"As you would," says Christ, "that men should do to you, do you also to them in like manner."[88]

271. **What particular duties are required of me by that rule?**

Never to injure your neighbor by word or deed, in his person, property, or character: to wish well to him, and to pray for him; and always to assist him, as far as you are able, in his spiritual and corporal necessities.

---

[85] Cf. Mt 5:28
[86] Lk 10:27-28; Cf. Mk 12:28-34
[87] Lk 10:29
[88] Lk 6:31

272. **Am I also obliged to love my enemies?**

Most certainly. "Love your enemies," says Christ, "do good to them that hate you, bless them that curse you, and pray for them that persecute and calumniate you.[89]

Chapter 7

LESSON 20

On the Precepts of the Church

273. **Are there any other commandments, besides the ten commandments of God?**

There are the commandments or precepts of the Church, which are chiefly six.

274. **Say the six commandments of the Church.**
   1. To hear Mass on Sundays, and all holy days of obligation.
   2. To fast and abstain on the days commanded.
   3. To confess our sins at least once a year.
   4. To receive worthily the Blessed Eucharist at Easter, or within the time appointed.
   5. To contribute to the support of our pastors.
   6. Not to solemnize marriage at the forbidden times, nor to marry persons within the forbidden degrees of kindred, or otherwise prohibited by the Church, nor clandestinely.

[89] Lk 6:27-28; Mt 5:44

275. **What is our first and chief duty on Sundays and holy days?**

To hear Mass devoutly; and in every other respect we should keep them holy.

276. **Is it a mortal sin not to hear Mass on a Sunday or holy day?**

It is, if the omission be culpable; and fathers and mothers, masters and mistresses, and all such persons, sin grievously, who hinder, without sufficient cause, children, servants, or any others subject to them, from hearing Mass on a Sunday or holy day.[90]

277. **What do you mean by holy days?**

Certain solemn days ordered by the Church to be kept holy.

278. **Why were holy days instituted by the Church?**

To recall to our minds, with praise and thanksgiving, the great mysteries of religion; and the virtues and rewards of the saints, and to glorify God on them.

279. **How are we to keep holy days?**

As we should keep the Sundays.

280. **What are we obliged to do by the second commandment of the Church?**

To give part of the year to fast and abstinence.[91]

281. **What do you mean by fast days?**

Certain days on which we are allowed but one meal, and forbidden flesh meat.

282. **What do you mean by days of abstinence?**

Certain days on which we are forbidden to eat flesh meat; but are allowed the usual number of meals.

---

[90] Cf. 2 Thes 3:4, 14
[91] Cf. Mt 6:16-18

283. **Why does the Church command us to fast and abstain?**
To mortify our sinful passions and appetites; and to satisfy for our sins, by doing penance for them.

284. **Is it strictly forbidden by the Church to eat flesh meat on days of abstinence?**
Yes; and to eat flesh meat on any day on which it is forbidden, without necessity and leave from the Church, is very sinful.

285. **Why does the Church command us to abstain from flesh meat on Fridays?**
In honor and commemoration of our Savior's death.

LESSON 21

The Precepts of the Church Continued

286. **What means the commandment of confessing our sins, at least once a year?**
It means that we are threatened with very severe penalties by the Church, if we do not go to confession within the year.

287. **Does a bad confession satisfy the obligation of confessing our sins once a year?**
So far from it, that it renders us more guilty by the additional crime of sacrilege.

288. **Is it sufficient to go but once a year to confession?**
No; frequent confession is necessary for all those who fall into mortal sin, or who desire to advance in virtue.

289. **At what age are children obliged to go to confession?**
As soon as they are capable of committing sin, that is, when they come to the use of reason; which is generally supposed to be about the age of seven years.

290. **At what age are children obliged to receive the Blessed Eucharist?**
As soon as they are able to discern the body of the Lord; that is, when they understand what the Blessed Eucharist is, and how they should be prepared to receive it worthily.[92]

291. **What punishment has the Church decreed against those who neglect to receive the Blessed Eucharist at Easter?**
They are to be excluded from the house of God whilst living, and deprived of Christian burial when they die.[93]

292. **Are we obliged in conscience and justice to contribute to the support of our pastors?**
Yes; and by a divine precept also. St. Paul says, "So the Lord ordained that they who preach the gospel should live by the gospel."[94]

293. **Do the precepts of the Church oblige under pain of mortal sin?**
Yes; "He that will not hear the church," says Christ, "let him be to thee as the heathen and the publican."[95]

294. **What is necessary to keep the commandments of God, and of his Church?**
The grace of God, which is to be obtained chiefly by prayer and the sacraments.

[92] Cf. 1 Cor 11:29
[93] Cf. Fourth Lateran Council, Const. 21
[94] 1 Cor 9:13-14
[95] Mt 18:17; Cf. Lk 10:16

Chapter 8

LESSON 22

On Prayer

295. What is prayer?

An elevation of the soul to God, to adore him, to bless his holy name, to praise his goodness, and to return him thanks for his benefits.

296. Is prayer anything else?

It is a humble petition to God for all necessaries, for soul and body.

297. When should we pray?

Christ himself says, "We ought always to pray."[96]

298. How can we always pray?

By offering to God all our thoughts, words, and actions; by keeping ourselves in the state of grace; and by praying at certain times.

299. At what particular time should we pray?

On Sundays and holy days; every morning and every night; and in all dangers, temptations, and affliction.

300. After what manner should we pray?

With all possible attention and devotion; and in a respectful posture on bended knees.

301. What conditions are necessary to render our prayers acceptable?

We must always offer them with a humble and contrite heart; with fervor

---

[96] Lk 18:1

and perseverance; with confidence in God's goodness; with resignation to his will, and in the name of Jesus Christ.

302. **What do you say of those, who, at their prayers, think not of God, nor of what they say?**
If their distractions be willful, their prayers, instead of pleasing God, offend him.[97]

303. **What prayers are most recommended to us?**
The Lord's Prayer, the Hail Mary, the Apostles' Creed, and the *confiteor*, or general confession.

304. **Does the Church also recommend the acts of faith, hope, and charity?**
Yes, most earnestly. They are an excellent form of prayer, and remind us of our chief duties to God.

305. **What are our chief duties to God?**
To believe in him, to hope in him, and to love him.

306. **Why do you make an act of contrition before the acts of faith, hope and charity?**
To obtain pardon of my sins: and thereby to render my prayers more acceptable to God, and more beneficial to myself.

LESSON 23

On the Lord's Prayer and Hail Mary

307. **Who made the Lord's Prayer?**
Jesus Christ.[98]

---

[97] Cf. Jas 1:6
[98] Cf. Mt 6:9-13

308. Whom do you call "Our Father," when you say the Lord's Prayer?
Almighty God, who is the common Father of all.[99]

309. What means, "Hallowed be thy name"?
By this we beg, that God's name may be praised and glorified by all his creatures.

310. What means, "Thy kingdom come"?
By this we beg, that God may reign in our hearts by his grace, in this life; and that we may reign forever with him, in the next.

311. What means, "Thy will be done"?
By this we beg, that God would enable us, by his grace, to do his will in all things on earth, as the angels and saints do it in heaven.

312. What means, "Give us this day our daily bread"?
By this we beg for all necessaries, for our souls and bodies.

313. What means, "Forgive us our trespasses, as we forgive them who trespass against us"?
By this we beg, that God would forgive our offenses, as we forgive them who offend us.

314. Will God forgive our offenses, if we do not forgive our enemies, and all those who have offended us?
No; God will show no mercy to us, unless we forgive from our hearts, our enemies, and all those who have offended or injured us.[100]

315. What means, "Lead us not into temptation"?
By this we beg, that God would strengthen us against all temptations.[101]

[99] Cf. 1 Jn 3:1
[100] Cf. Mt 18:35; 6:15
[101] Cf. 1 Cor 10:13

316. **What means, "Deliver us from evil"?**

By this we beg, that God would deliver us, in body and soul, from all evil, particularly that of sin.

317. **Who made the Hail Mary?**

The angel Gabriel and Saint Elizabeth made the first part of it;[102] and the Church made the last.

318. **Is it lawful to honor the Virgin Mary?**

Yes; whereas God himself so much honored her; and the scripture says, "all nations shall call (her) blessed."[103]

319. **What honor do we give our Blessed Lady?**

We honor her more than all the other saints, because she is the Mother of God; but we never give her divine or supreme honor, which is due to God alone.

320. **Why do Catholics so often repeat the Hail Mary and Holy Mary?**

To honor the mystery of the incarnation, which that prayer expresses; and to show their great respect and devotion to the Mother of God, and their special confidence in her assistance, particularly at the hour of death.

321. **And why do you always say the Hail Mary after the Lord's Prayer?**

That, by her intercession, we may more easily obtain what we ask for in the Lord's Prayer.

---

[102] Cf. Lk 1:28, 42
[103] Lk 1:48

Chapter 9

LESSON 24

On the Sacraments, and on Baptism

322. **By what other means, besides prayer, can we obtain the grace of God?**
By the sacraments, the most powerful of all means.

323. **What is a sacrament?**
A visible, that is, an outward sign or action, instituted by Christ, to give grace.

324. **Whence have the sacraments the power of giving grace?**
From the merits of Christ, which they apply to our souls.[104]

325. **Why are so many ceremonies used in the administration of the sacraments?**
To excite devotion, and reverence to them; and to signify and explain their effects.

326. **How many sacraments are there?**
Seven: baptism, confirmation, Eucharist, penance, extreme unction, holy order, and matrimony.[105]

327. **What is baptism?**
A sacrament, which cleanses us from original sin, makes us Christians and children of God, and heirs to the kingdom of heaven.

---

[104] Cf. Rom 6:3; 5:9
[105] Cf. Council of Trent, Session 7, Can. 1

328. **Does baptism also remit the actual sins committed before it?**

Yes; and all the punishment due to them.

329. **Is baptism necessary to salvation?**

Yes; without it one "cannot enter into the kingdom of God."[106]

330. **Who are appointed by Christ to give baptism?**

The pastors of his Church; but in case of necessity, any layman or woman can give it.

331. **How is baptism given?**

By pouring water on the head of the person to be baptized; saying at the same time, "I baptize thee, in the name of the Father, and of the Son, and of the Holy Ghost."[107]

332. **What did we promise in baptism?**

To renounce the devil, with all his works and pomps.

LESSON 25

On Confirmation

333. **What is confirmation?**

A sacrament, which makes us strong and perfect Christians.[108]

334. **How does the bishop give confirmation?**

By the imposition of hands and by prayer; that is, he holds out his hands, and prays at the same time, that the Holy Ghost may descend upon those who are to be confirmed—and then he makes the sign of the cross on their foreheads with chrism.

[106] Jn 3:5
[107] Cf. Mt 28:19
[108] Cf. 2 Cor 1:22; Acts 8:14-16

335. **Why does the bishop give the persons he confirms a stroke on the cheek?**
To put them in mind, that by confirmation they are strengthened to suffer; and, if necessary, even to die for Christ.

336. **To receive confirmation, worthily, is it necessary to be in the state of grace?**
Yes; and children of an age to learn should be instructed in the Christian doctrine.

337. **What special preparations should be made for confirmation?**
You should make a good confession; and by fervent prayer, beseech your heavenly Father to send his Holy Spirit on you.[109]

338. **What do you think of those who receive confirmation in the state of mortal sin?**
They receive no benefit by it—but become more sinful, by adding to their former guilt the horrid crime of sacrilege.

339. **What graces are received by confirmation?**
The seven gifts of the Holy Ghost.

340. **Repeat the seven gifts of the Holy Ghost.**
Wisdom, understanding, counsel, fortitude, knowledge, piety, and the fear of the Lord.

341. **What obligations do we contract by confirmation?**
To profess our faith openly, not to deny our religion on any occasion whatsoever, and, like good soldiers of Christ, to be faithful to him unto death.[110]

[109] Cf. Lk 11:13
[110] Cf. Apoc 2:10

342. **Is it a sin to neglect confirmation?**

Yes; especially in these evil days, when faith and morals are exposed to so many, and such violent temptations.

LESSON 26

On the Blessed Eucharist

343. **What is the Blessed Eucharist?**

The body and blood, soul and divinity of Jesus Christ, under the appearance of bread and wine.

344. **What means the word *eucharist*?**

A special grace or gift of God; and it means also a solemn act of thanksgiving to God for all his mercies.

345. **What do you mean by the appearances of bread and wine?**

The taste, color, and form of bread and wine, which still remain, after the bread and wine are changed into the body and blood of Christ.

346. **Are both the body and blood of Christ under the appearance of bread and under the appearance of wine?**

Yes; Christ is whole and entire, true God and true man, under the appearance of each.

347. **Are we to believe that the God of all glory is under the appearance of our corporal food?**

Yes; as we also believe that the same God of all glory suffered death, under the appearance of a criminal on the cross.

348. **How can the bread and wine become the body and blood of Christ?**
By the goodness and power of God, with whom "no word shall be impossible."[111]

349. **Are we assured that Christ changed bread and wine into his body and blood?**
Yes; by the very words which Christ himself said, when he instituted the Blessed Eucharist at his last supper.

350. **Which are the words Christ said, when he instituted the Blessed Eucharist?**
"This is my body… this is my blood."[112]

351. **Did Christ give power to the priests of his Church, to change bread and wine into his body and blood?**
Yes; when he said to his apostles at his last supper: "Do this for a commemoration of me."[113]

352. **Why did Christ give to the priests of his Church so great a power?**
That his children, throughout all ages and nations, might have a most acceptable sacrifice to offer to their heavenly Father—and the most precious food to nourish their souls.

353. **What is a sacrifice?**
That first and most necessary act of religion, whereby we acknowledge God's supreme dominion over us, and our total dependence on him.

354. **What is the sacrifice of the new law?**
The Mass.

355. **What is the Mass?**
The sacrifice of the body and blood of Christ, which are really present

[111] Lk 1:37
[112] Mt 26:26, 28
[113] Lk 22:19

under the appearances of bread and wine; and are offered to God by the priest for the living and the dead.

356. **Is the Mass a different sacrifice from that of the cross?**

No; because the same Christ, who once offered himself a bleeding victim to his heavenly Father on the cross, continues to offer himself, in an unbloody manner, by the hands of his priests, on our altars.

357. **Was Mass offered in the old law?**

No; so great a sacrifice was reserved for the new law, which was to fulfill the figures of the old law, and to give religion its full perfection.

358. **At what part of the Mass are the bread and wine changed into the body and blood of Christ?**

At the consecration.

359. **By whom are the bread and wine changed into the body and blood of Christ?**

By the priest; but in virtue of the words of Christ, whose Person the priest represents, at the awful moment of consecration.

360. **What are the ends for which Mass is said?**

To give God honor and glory; to thank him for his benefits; to obtain the remission of our sins and all other graces and blessings through Jesus Christ.

361. **For what other end is Mass offered?**

To continue and represent the sacrifice of Christ on the cross. "This do," says Christ, "for the commemoration of me."[114]

---

[114] 1 Cor 11:24

362. **How should we assist at Mass?**

With great interior recollection and piety, and with every mark of outward respect and devotion.

363. **Which is the best manner of hearing Mass?**

To offer it to God with the priest for the same purposes for which it is said; to meditate on Christ's sufferings; and to go to Communion.

LESSON 27

On Communion and Penance

364. **What do you mean by going to Communion?**

Receiving the Blessed Eucharist.

365. **Is it advisable to go often to Communion?**

It is; as nothing can conduce more to a holy life. "He that eateth this bread," says Christ, "shall live forever."[115]

366. **How must we be prepared for Communion?**

We must be in the state of grace; penetrated with a lively faith, animated with a firm hope, and inflamed with an ardent charity.[116]

367. **What means to be in the state of grace?**

To be free, at least, from the guilt of mortal sin.

368. **How are we to be penetrated with a lively faith?**

By firmly believing that the Blessed Eucharist is Jesus Christ himself, true God and true man, his very flesh and blood, with his soul and divinity.

---

[115] Jn 6:59
[116] Cf. 1 Cor 11:28

369. **How are we to be animated with a firm hope?**

By having great confidence in the goodness of Christ, who gives himself to us without reserve, in that banquet of love.

370. **And how are we to be inflamed with ardent charity?**

By returning love for love to Christ, and by devoting ourselves in earnest to his service, all the days of our lives.

371. **Is anything else required before Communion?**

Yes. to be fasting from midnight; and we should appear very modest and humble, and clean in dress, showing in our whole exterior the greatest devotion and reverence to so holy a sacrament.

372. **What should we do after Communion?**

We should spend some time in meditation and prayer; and particularly in acts of thanksgiving.

373. **Is it a great sin to receive it unworthily?**

Yes. Whosoever receives unworthily, shall be guilty of the body and of the blood of the Lord; and eats judgment, that is, damnation to himself, not discerning the body of the Lord.[117]

374. **What do you mean by receiving unworthily?**

To receive the Blessed Eucharist in the state of mortal sin.

375. **What should a person do if he be in mortal sin before Communion?**

He must obtain pardon in the sacrament of penance.

376. **What is penance?**

A sacrament, by which the sins are forgiven, which are committed after baptism.

---

[117] Cf. 1 Cor 11:27-29

377. **By whose power are sins forgiven?**

By the power of God, which Christ left to the pastors of his Church.

378. **When did Christ leave to the pastors of his Church the power of forgiving sins?**

Chiefly when he said to his apostles, "Receive ye the Holy Ghost: whose sins you shall forgive, they are forgiven them: and whose sins you shall retain, they are retained."[118]

379. **What must we do, to obtain pardon of our sins in the sacrament of penance?**

We must make a good confession.

LESSON 28

On Confession, and on Indulgence

380. **What is the best method to prepare for a good confession?**

First, earnestly to beg of God the grace to make a good confession. Secondly, to examine ourselves, carefully, on the commandments of God and of his Church, on the seven deadly sins, and particularly on our predominant passions and the duties of our stations in life: that we may know in what and how often we have sinned by thought, word, deed, or omission. Thirdly, to make acts of faith, hope, and charity. And fourthly, to excite ourselves to sincere contrition for our sins.

381. **What is contrition?**

A hearty sorrow and detestation of sin, for having offended God, with a firm resolution of sinning no more.

382. **How may we excite ourselves to contrition?**

By the following motives or considerations: the fear of hell; the loss of

---

[118] Jn 20:22-23

heaven; our ingratitude in offending God, who is so good to us; and the injury our sins do to God, who is infinitely good in himself.

383. **Do you recommend any other motive to excite sorrow for our sins?**
Yes; to consider that the son of God died for our sins, and that we crucify him again as often as we offend him.[119]

384. **Which of these motives is the best to excite contrition?**
To be sorry for our sins because they are offensive to God, who is infinitely good and perfect in himself.

385. **What should we do at confession?**
We should beg the priest's blessing; say the *confiteor*; accuse ourselves of our sins; listen attentively to his instructions; and renew our sorrow, when he gives absolution.

386. **What do you think of those who conceal a mortal sin in confession?**
They commit a most grievous sin by telling a lie to the Holy Ghost[120]—and instead of obtaining pardon, they incur much more the wrath of God.

387. **What must persons do who did not carefully examine their conscience; or who had not sincere sorrow for their sins; or who willfully concealed a mortal sin in confession?**
They must truly repent of all such bad and sacrilegious confessions; and make them all over again.

388. **What is the surest sign that our confessions were good; and that we had a sincere sorrow for our sins?**
The amendment of our lives.

[119] Cf. Heb 6:6
[120] Cf. Acts 5:1-5

389. **What should we do after confession?**
We should return God thanks; and diligently perform the penance enjoined by the confessor.

390. **What do you mean by the penance enjoined by the confessor?**
The prayers and other good works which he enjoins on penitents, in satisfaction for their sins.

391. **Will the penance, enjoined in confession, always satisfy for our sins?**
No; but whatever else is wanting may be supplied by indulgences, and our own penitential endeavors.

392. **What does the Church teach concerning indulgences?**
That Christ gave power to the Church to grant indulgences; and that they are most useful to Christian people.[121]

393. **What is the use of an indulgence?**
It releases from canonical penance, enjoined by the Church on penitents, for certain sins.

394. **Has an indulgence any other effect?**
It also remits the temporary punishments, with which God often visits our sins—and which must be suffered in this life, or the next; unless cancelled by indulgences, by act of penance, or other good works.

395. **Has the Church power to grant such indulgences?**
Yes; "Whatsoever," says Christ to St. Peter, "thou shalt loose upon earth, it shall be loosed also in heaven."[122]

---

[121] Cf. Council of Trent, Session 25, Ch. 21
[122] Mt 16:19; Cf. 2 Cor 2:10

396. **To whom does the Church grant indulgences?**

To such only as are in the state of grace; and are sincerely desirous to amend their lives; and to satisfy God's justice by penitential works.

397. **An indulgence is not then a pardon for sins to come nor license to commit sin?**

No; nor can it remit past sin. For sin must be remitted by penance, as to the guilt of it, and the eternal punishment due to mortal sin, before an indulgence can be gained.[123]

398. **Why does the Church grant indulgences?**

To assist our weakness, and to supply our insufficiency in satisfying the divine justice for our transgressions.

399. **What conditions are generally necessary to gain indulgences?**

A good confession and communion, and a faithful compliance with the other good works, which the Church requires on such occasions.

400. **What are the other good works, which the Church usually prescribes, in order to gain indulgences?**

Prayer, fast, and almsdeeds; which good works indulgences promote; and on this account also they are most useful to Christian people.

LESSON 29

On Extreme Unction, Holy Orders, and Matrimony

401. **What is extreme unction?**

A sacrament which gives grace to die well; and is instituted chiefly for the spiritual strength and comfort of dying persons.

---

[123] Cf. 1 Cor 5; 2 Cor 2

402. **Is extreme unction given to all persons in danger of death?**

No; only to such as are in danger of death by sickness.

403. **How should we prepare ourselves for extreme unction?**

By a good confession—and we should be truly sorry for our sins, and resigned to the will of God, when we are receiving that last sacrament.

404. **Who are appointed to administer the sacrament of extreme unction?**

The priests of the Church, as St. James teaches, and as the Church has constantly practiced. "Is any man sick among you? Let him bring in the priests of the church, and let them pray over him, anointing him with oil in the name of the Lord,"[124] etc.

405. **What is holy order?**

A sacrament, which gives bishops, priests, and inferior clergy to the Church; and enables them to perform their several duties in it.[125]

406. **What is matrimony?**

A sacrament, which gives grace to the husband and wife to live happy together; and to bring up their children in the fear and love of God.[126]

407. **Do they receive the grace of the sacrament of matrimony who contract marriage in the state of mortal sin?**

No; they are guilty of a very great sacrilege, by profaning so great a sacrament;[127] and instead of a blessing, they receive their condemnation.

408. **What should persons do to receive worthily the sacrament of marriage?**

They should make a good confession—and earnestly beseech God to grant them a pure intention, and to direct them in the choice they are to make.

[124] Jas 5:14-15
[125] Cf. Phil 1:1
[126] Cf. Mt 19:6
[127] Cf. Eph 5:32

409. **Should children consult their parents on their intended marriages?**

Yes; and be advised by them according to reason and religion—they should also give timely notice to their pastor.

410. **What is the reason that so many marriages prove unhappy?**

Because many enter into that holy state from unworthy motives, and with guilty consciences: therefore their marriages are not blessed by God.

411. **Can the bond or tie of marriage be ever broken?**

It never can, but by the death of the husband or wife.[128]

412. **Can the sacraments be received more than once?**

All can, except baptism, confirmation, and holy orders, which imprint on the soul a character, or spiritual mark, which never can be effaced.

413. **Which sacraments are most necessary to us?**

Baptism and penance.

414. **Why did Christ institute the sacraments?**

For the sanctification of our souls, and to prepare us for a happy and glorious resurrection.

---

[128] Cf. Mt 19:3-9; Rom 7:1-3; 1 Cor 7

Chapter 10

LESSON 30

On the General Judgment

415. **What means the resurrection of the body?**

That we shall all rise again, on the last day, with the same bodies which we had in this life.

416. **What do you mean by the last day?**

The day of general judgment, when we must all be manifested before the judgment seat of Christ, and then will he render to every man according to his works.[129]

417. **Will our bodies rise united to our souls?**

Yes; to share in the soul's eternal bliss or misery.

418. **How are the bodies of the saints to rise?**

Glorious and immortal.

419. **Are the bodies of the damned to rise glorious?**

No; but they shall rise immortal, to live forever in eternal flames.

420. **In what manner will Christ come to judge us?**

"In the clouds of heaven," attended by many legions of angels, and "with great power and majesty."[130]

---

[129] Cf. 2 Cor 5:10; Mt 16:27
[130] Mt 24:30

421. **As everyone is judged immediately after death, what need is there of a general judgment?**
That the providence of God, which often here permits the good to suffer, and the wicked to prosper, may appear just before all men.

422. **What will Christ say to the good on the last day?**
"Come, ye blessed of my Father, possess the kingdom prepared for you."[131]

423. **What shall Christ say to the wicked on the last day?**
"Depart from me, ye cursed, into everlasting fire, which was prepared for the devil and his angels."[132]

424. **Where must the wicked go at the last day?**
They "shall go," both body and soul, "into everlasting punishment."[133]

425. **And where shall the just go at the last day?**
"The just" will enter, with glorious and immortal bodies, "into life everlasting."[134]

426. **What means life everlasting?**
It means, if we serve God faithfully in this life, we shall be happy with him forever in heaven.

427. **What is the happiness of heaven?**
To see, love, and enjoy God, in the kingdom of his glory, forever and ever. Amen.

428. **What means Amen?**
So be it.

[131] Mt 25:34
[132] Mt 25:41
[133] Mt 25:46
[134] Ibid.

On the Rule of Faith

429. What is the Catholic rule of faith?[135]

The revealed word of God.

430. Of what does the revealed word of God consist?

It consists of two parts: the written word, called the holy scripture, and the unwritten word, called divine tradition.

431. Are these two parts of equal authority?

Yes; because they have been equally revealed by God.

432. Which of these parts was before the other?

The unwritten word was before the written word, with respect both to the old testament and the new testament.

433. What divine traditions existed before Moses wrote the first books of the old testament?

The duty of sanctifying the sabbath,[136] the prohibition of eating the blood of animals,[137] the rite of circumcision,[138] and generally, the whole history of religion before the time of Moses, during two thousand five hundred years.

434. What traditions of the Christian religion existed before the several books of the new testament were promulgated or written?

The substitution of the Sunday, as a holy day, for the sabbath, or Saturday; the abrogation of the necessity of circumcision; and, generally, the whole system of the Christian religion.

---

[135] Editor's Note: Questions 429-452 originally comprised an appendix entitled "The Catholic Scriptural Catechism, by the Rt. Rev. Dr. Milner."

[136] Cf. Gn 2:3

[137] Cf. Gn 9:4

[138] Cf. Gn 17:10

435. Did Jesus Christ write the new scripture?

No, he did not write any part of it.

436. Did he at any time before his ascension, command his apostles to write it?

No: though some of them were inspired, on subsequent occasions, to write the books of it, which bear their names.

437. In what manner then did Christ commission them to publish his doctrine and precepts?

By preaching; his last words to them, according to St. Matthew, being these: "Going, therefore, teach ye all nations, baptizing them in the name of the Father, and of the Son, and of the Holy Ghost; teaching them to observe all things, whatsoever I have commanded you: and, behold, I am with you all days, even to the consummation of the world."[139]

438. Did the apostles observe this precept in converting nations to the faith?

Yes, they did: for St. Mark testifies of them, that after Christ had commanded them to "preach the gospel to every creature... they, going forth, preached everywhere; the Lord working withal, and confirming the word by signs that followed."[140]

439. Did the apostles instruct their disciples to follow the same method?

Yes; for St. Paul writes to Timothy: "The things which thou hast heard of me by many witnesses, the same commend to faithful men, who shall be fit to teach others also."[141]

440. Has no Christian nation or province, since the time of the apostles, been converted by reading the holy scriptures?

No: they have all been converted by preachers, succeeding, by due authority, to the above-mentioned commission, given to the apostles.

---

[139] Mt 28:19-20
[140] Mk 16:15, 20
[141] 2 Tm 2:2

441. **Did not Christ tell the Jews to "search the scriptures,"[142] and did not St. Paul commend the Bereans for "searching the scriptures, whether these things were so"?[143]**

The texts in both these instances referred to the prophecies in the old testament concerning the Messiah, which were evidently fulfilled in the Person and actions of our Savior; not to the doctrines of Christianity, nor to the new testament, which was not then written. The same is to be said of St. Paul's commendation of Timothy, for having known the holy scriptures from his infancy.[144] Reading the old testament with suitable disposition, no doubt was profitable to this disciple for instruction; but the apostle plainly signifies that Timothy had learnt his faith in Jesus Christ from him, St. Paul,[145] namely, when he preached at Lystra.[146]

442. **Are the scriptures, of themselves, easy to be understood?**

No: they contain "things hard to be understood, which the unlearned and unstable wrest...to their own destruction."[147] The same is evident from the great variety of sects, who profess to build their faith on the scriptures alone, and yet differ from each other on the fundamental articles of Christianity.

443. **Has Christ furnished us with any means by which we may learn with certainty, the sense of the holy scripture in all necessary points?**

Yes; he has established a never-failing tribunal, both to preserve and to interpret his divine word in both its branches, namely, his holy Church.

444. **How do you prove this?**

In every state and society of mankind, there are and must be judges and magistrates, to maintain the laws, and to decide upon their meaning.

[142] Jn 5:39
[143] Acts 17:11
[144] Cf. 2 Tm 3:15
[145] Cf. 2 Tm 3:14-15
[146] Cf. Acts 14:6
[147] 2 Pt 3:16

Accordingly Christ, in founding his Church, against which "the gates of hell shall not prevail,"[148] commands us all to hear it, under pain of being considered as heathens and publicans.[149] In like manner, having sent his apostles to "teach all nations,"[150] he promised to remain with them forever,[151] and to send them the Spirit of truth which shall teach them all truth.[152]

445. How does the Church deliver to us the sense of scripture and tradition?

By the decisions of her bishops, and especially of her chief bishop in the chair of St. Peter; by the sermons and instructions of her other pastors, and by the approved good books, especially the catechisms, which she puts into our hands.

446. Is it not morally possible that the doctrines of the seven sacraments, the real presence, transubstantiation, invoking the saints, praying for the dead, etc., which Catholics term divine traditions, and the true sense of scripture, may have sprung from the fraud of the clergy, and the credulity of the people, at some former period?

No; this is morally impossible: since these doctrines have always been held, both by the clergy and people of the whole Catholic Church, spread, as it is, and always has been, throughout the whole world. Besides this, these doctrines are, and always have been, held by the ancient heretics, who were separated from the Catholic Church in the fifth and the following centuries.

447. In what does the word of God, contained in the holy scriptures, properly consist?

Not in the mere words of the sacred text: but in the meaning of it, as the holy fathers teach.

---

[148] Mt 16:18
[149] Cf. Mt 18:17
[150] Mt 28:19
[151] Cf. Mt 28:20
[152] Cf. Jn 16:13

448. **What follows from this?**

That many persons who are the most assiduous in reading the Bible, yet do not attain to the truths of religion, taught by Jesus Christ, and are really ignorant of the word of God.

449. **What else?**

That others who have learned the essential truths of revelation, as to what they have to believe, and what they have to practice, from their pastor's instructions and their catechisms, have really attained to the knowledge of God's word, even though they should never have read any portion of the Bible.

450. **Is there any obligation of reading the scriptures?**

The Catholic clergy are required to read and to pray out of it every day. A more strict obligation of studying both the written and the unwritten word of God lies on the pastors, whose duty it is to inculcate it to the faithful. But there is no such general obligation incumbent on the laity: it being sufficient that they listen to it from their pastors.

451. **Is it lawful for the laity to read the holy scriptures?**

They may read them in the language in which they were written, as likewise in the ancient vulgate translation, which the Church vouches to be authentic. They may also read them in approved modern versions; but with due submission to the interpretation and authority of the Church.

452. **Have any great evils ensued from an unrestricted reading of the Bible, in vulgar languages, by the unlearned and unstable?**

Yes; numberless heresies and impieties; as also many rebellions and civil wars.

Of Exorcisms, and Benedictions, or Blessings of Creatures in the Catholic Church, and of the Use of Holy Water

453. What do you mean by exorcism?[153]

The rites and prayers instituted by the Church for casting out devils, or restraining them from hurting persons, disquieting places, or abusing any of God's creatures to our harm.

454. Has Christ given his Church any such power over the devils?

Yes he has. This power was given to the apostles,[154] and to the seventy-two disciples,[155] and to other believers.[156] And that this power was not to die with the apostles, nor to cease after the apostolic age, we learn from the perpetual practice of the Church and the experience of all ages.

455. What is the meaning of blessing so many things in the Catholic Church?

We bless churches and other places set aside for divine service, altars, chalices, vestments, etc., by way of devoting them to holy uses. We bless our meats and other inanimate things which God has given us for our use, that we may use them with moderation, in a manner agreeable to God's institution; that they may be serviceable to us, and that the devil may have no power to abuse them to our prejudice. We bless candles, salt, water, etc., by way of begging of God that such as religiously use them may obtain his blessing, etc.

456. But does it not favor of superstition to attribute any virtue to such inanimate things as blessed candles, holy water, agnus dei's, etc.?

It is no superstition to look for a good effect from the prayers of the Church of God; and it is in virtue of these prayers that we hope for benefit from

---

[153] Editor's Note: Questions 453-463 are taken directly from Bishop Richard Challoner's *Catholick Christian Instructed* (1737), included in Volume III of this series.

[154] Cf. Mt 10:1; Mk 3:15; Lk 9:1

[155] Cf. Lk 10:19

[156] Cf. Mk 16:17

these things, when used with faith; and daily experience shows that our hopes are not vain.

457. **What do you mean by agnus dei's?**
Wax stamped with the image of the Lamb of God, blessed by the pope with solemn prayers, and anointed with the holy chrism.

458. **What warrant have you in scripture for blessing inanimate things?**
"Every creature of God is good, and nothing to be refused, if it be received with thanksgiving: for it is sanctified by the word of God and prayer."[157]

459. **Why does the Church make use of the sign of the cross in all her blessings and consecrations?**
To signify that all our good must come through Christ crucified.

460. **What do you mean by holy water?**
Water sanctified by the word of God and prayer.

461. **What is the use of holy water?**
It is blessed by the Church with solemn prayers, to beg God's protection and blessing upon those that use it, and in particular that they may be defended from all the powers of darkness.

462. **Is the use of holy water very ancient in the Church of God?**
It is very ancient, since it is mentioned in the *Apostolic Constitutions*.[158] And as for our English nation in particular, it is visible from the epistles of St. Gregory the Great that we received it together with our Christianity.[159]

---

[157] 1 Tm 4:4-5
[158] Cf. *Apostolic Constitutions*, Bk. 8, Ch. 29
[159] Cf. Gregory the Great, *Epistola ad Mellitum*

463. **Have the holy fathers and ancient Church writers left upon record any miracles done by holy water?**

Yes they have; more particularly upon those occasions when it has been used against magical enchantments and the power of the devil.[160]

Of Christian Virtues and Good Works

464. **Say the three theological virtues.**

Faith, hope, and charity.

465. **What is charity?**

It is a divine virtue, whereby we love God for himself, and our neighbor for God.

466. **Say the four cardinal virtues.**

Prudence, justice, temperance, and fortitude.

467. **How many sorts of alms or works of mercy are there?**

Two: corporal and spiritual.

468. **How many corporal works of mercy?**

Seven:

1. To feed the hungry.
2. To give drink to the thirsty.
3. To clothe the naked.
4. To harbor pilgrims or travelers.
5. To ransom prisoners.
6. To visit the sick.
7. To bury the dead.

---

[160] Cf. Epiphanius, *Haeresi 30*; Jerome, *Life of St. Hilarion*; Theodoret, *Ecclesiastical History*, Bk. 5, Ch. 21; Palladius, *The Lausiac History*, Ch. 17

469. How many spiritual works of mercy?

Seven:

1. To give good counsel.
2. To instruct the ignorant.
3. To admonish sinners.
4. To comfort the afflicted.
5. To pardon injuries.
6. To bear wrongs patiently.
7. To pray for the living and the dead.

470. The Eight Beatitudes

1. Blessed are the poor in spirit, for theirs is the kingdom of heaven.
2. Blessed are the meek, for they shall possess the earth.
3. Blessed are they that mourn, for they shall be comforted.
4. Blessed are they that hunger and thirst after justice, for they shall be filled.
5. Blessed are the merciful, for they shall obtain mercy.
6. Blessed are the clean of heart, for they shall see God.
7. Blessed are the peacemakers, for they shall be called the children of God.
8. Blessed are they that suffer persecution for righteousness sake, for theirs is the kingdom of heaven.

The Fifteen Mysteries of the Rosary

471. Say the five joyful mysteries.

1. The annunciation of our Lady when the Son of God was conceived.
2. The visitation of St. Elizabeth.
3. The nativity of our Lord Jesus Christ.
4. The presentation of our Lord in the Temple.
5. The finding of our Lord in the Temple among the doctors.

472. Say the five sorrowful mysteries.
1. The prayer of our Lord in the garden.
2. The whipping him at the pillar.
3. The crowning him with a crown of thorns.
4. His carrying of the cross to Mount Calvary.
5. His crucifixion and death on the cross.

473. Say the five glorious mysteries.
1. The resurrection of our Lord.
2. His ascension into heaven.
3. The coming of the Holy Ghost.
4. The assumption of our Lady into heaven.
5. Her coronation above all angels and saints.

Appendix

The Ten Commandments of God as Found in the 20th Chapter of Exodus

And the Lord spoke all these words: I am the Lord thy God, who brought thee out of the land of Egypt, out of the house of bondage. Thou shalt not have strange gods before me. Thou shalt not make to thyself a graven thing, nor the likeness of any thing that is in heaven above, or in the earth beneath, nor of those things that are in the waters under the earth. Thou shalt not adore them, nor serve them. I am the Lord thy God, mighty, jealous, visiting the iniquity of the fathers upon the children, unto the third and fourth generation of them that hate me; and showing mercy unto thousands of them that love me, and keep my commandments. Thou shalt not take the name of the Lord thy God in vain: for the Lord will not hold him guiltless that shall take the name of the Lord his God in vain. Remember that thou keep holy the sabbath-day. Six days shalt thou labor, and shalt do all thy works. But on the seventh day is the sabbath of the Lord thy God: thou shalt do no work on it, then, nor thy son, nor thy daughter, nor thy man-servant, nor thy maid-servant, nor thy beast, nor the stranger that is within thy gates. For in six days the Lord made heaven and earth, and the sea, and all things that are in them, and rested on the seventh day: therefore the Lord blessed the seventh day and sanctified it. Honor thy father and thy mother, that thou mayst be long-lived upon the land which the Lord thy God will give thee. Thou shalt not kill. Thou shalt not commit adultery. Thou shalt not steal. Thou shalt not bear false witness against thy neighbor. Thou shalt not covet thy neighbor's house; neither shalt thou desire his wife, nor his servant, nor his handmaid, nor his ox, nor his ass, nor any thing that is his.

Holy Days of Obligation

Independently of Sundays, and feasts which fall upon them: the Circumcision of Our Lord; the Epiphany; the Annunciation of the Blessed Virgin; the Ascension; Corpus Christi, or the Feast of the Blessed Sacrament; The Assumption of the Blessed Virgin; All Saints; The Nativity of Our Lord.

Fasting Days

1. The forty days of Lent.
2. The Ember days at the four seasons, being the Wednesday, Friday, and Saturday, of the first week of Lent; of Whitsun-week, of the third week in September; and of the third week in Advent.
3. The Fridays of all the four weeks of Advent.
4. The Vigils or Eves of Whitsunday; of the Assumption of the Blessed Virgin; of All Saints; and of Christmas day.

N.B. Any fasting day, which falls on Sunday, is kept on the preceding Saturday.

Abstinence Days

All Fridays throughout the year. The abstinence on Saturday is dispensed with, for the faithful throughout the United States, for the space of twenty years, (from 1843,) except when a fast falls on Saturday. Hence, the Saturdays of Lent and Quartertenses, and vigils falling on Saturday, are still days of abstinence from flesh meat. When Christmas falls on Friday, abstinence is not of precept. All the Sundays in Lent are, by the general discipline of the Church, days of abstinence. The use of flesh meat is allowed at present, by dispensation, in this diocese, on all the Sundays of Lent, except Palm Sunday, and once a day on Monday, Tuesday, and Thursday in each week, except the Thursday after Ash Wednesday, and also excepting Holy Week.

N. B. The Catholic Church commands all her children, upon Sundays and holy days, to be present at the great Eucharistic Sacrifice, which we call the Mass, and to rest from servile work on those days, and keep them holy. Secondly, she commands them to abstain from flesh on all days of fasting and abstinence; and on fasting days, to eat but one meal. Thirdly, she commands them to confess their sins to their pastors, at least once a year. Fourthly, she commands them to receive the Blessed Sacrament at least once a year, and that at Easter, viz. between Palm Sunday and Low Sunday.

The Fourth Council of Lateran ordains, "that every one of the faithful of both sexes, after they come to the years of discretion, shall, in private, faithfully confess all their sins, at least once a year, to their own pastor, and take care to fulfill, to the best of their power, the penance enjoined them; receiving reverently, at least at Easter, the sacrament of the Eucharist, unless, perhaps, by the counsel of their pastor, for some reasonable cause, they judge it proper to abstain from it for a time; otherwise, let them be excluded from the Church while living, and when they die, be deprived of Christian burial."[161]

---

[161] Fourth Lateran Council, Const. 21

The Christian's Daily Exercise of Morning and Night Prayer

Rising from bed, make the sign of the cross, saying, "In the name of the Father, and of the Son, and of the Holy Ghost, Amen"—and offer yourself to God—then dressing yourself, modestly acknowledge the goodness of God, who gives you this day to labor in it, for the salvation of your soul; and consider this day may be your last. When dressed, place yourself in the presence of God, in a respectful posture, on bended knees, and blessing yourself, adore him with the most profound respect; give him thanks for his benefits to you, especially for having watched over you during the night; and join with all the angels and saints, in blessing and praising his holy name.

Afterwards recollect yourself, if you offended God during the night, and what were the sins you committed the day before; and with a humble and contrite heart, begging God's forgiveness of them and of all past transgressions, firmly resolve not to offend him anymore, and earnestly beg his assistance, to spend the present day in his love and service, and to guard you particularly against your predominant passions, and those vices, temptations, and failings, to which you find yourself most addicted.

Then offering to God your body and soul, with all your thoughts, words, and actions, and begging his blessing on them, devoutly recite the acts of faith, hope, and charity, the Lord's Prayer, the Hail Mary, the Apostles' Creed, and whatever other prayers you are accustomed to say. You should also pray for your friends and enemies, and for the living and dead, begging grace, mercy, and salvation for all mankind: and conclude your morning prayer by invoking the intercession and protection of the Blessed Virgin Mary; and by recommending yourself to your angel guardian, and to those particular saints, to whom you have spiritual devotion.

Every Christian, who has at heart his salvation, and is desirous to please God, ought, if he has time and opportunity, to meditate every morning, or at a convenient hour in the day, on his last end, or on the passion of Christ, or on some pious and serious subject; and to hear Mass with all possible attention and reverence; because of all religious duties, the Sacrifice of the Mass is that which gives most glory to God, and is at the same time most profitable to us; the reading of books of true Christian piety and sound morality is also earnestly to be recommended, as very conducive to spiritual improvement.

And in order to sanctify each day, and the good works of it, consider that "all things," even your most secret thoughts and actions "are naked and open" to the eyes of God;[162] and that "every idle word, that men shall speak, they shall render an account for it in the day of judgment."[163] Therefore walk with the greatest circumspection in the presence of God, frequently in the day thinking of him, raising your heart to him, and offering yourself and actions, to his honor and glory.

Night Prayer

If it be so necessary a duty to begin the day with prayer, it is of the utmost consequence to conclude it also by prayer; the graces received during the day, and special protection you stand in need of against the dangers of the night, should engage you, to humble yourself before God in prayer every night, which necessary duty is never to be omitted; and should be always most religiously performed, and in the same manner, and with the same dispositions, as in the morning.

Every night, therefore, before you go to bed, place yourself on your knees in the presence of God; and begging his blessing, by making the sign of the cross on yourself, adore his infinite majesty; return him thanks for all his mercies to you, especially for his gracious protection over you during the day; and invite the whole court of heaven and all the creatures of God, to bless his goodness, and to praise his holy name.

Then consider attentively, how you spent the day; and if in the course of it you diligently complied with your duty in every respect: you are therefore to examine yourself carefully on your thoughts, words, actions, and

---

[162] Heb 4:13
[163] Mt 12:36

omissions, and particularly on the obligations of your state in life, and on those vices, passions, and evil habits, to which you are most addicted.

When you have brought to mind all the sins and omissions of the day, with a humble and contrite heart implore forgiveness of them, and of all your transgressions; and firmly resolve, with God's assistance, not to offend him anymore; and cautiously to avoid every occasion of sin. Then offering yourself to God, earnestly beseech him to enable you to practice those particular virtues and good works, which are most necessary to you, and to preserve you from sin, and all dangers during the night; devoutly recite the acts of faith, hope, and charity, and the other prayers as in the morning, or any other form of prayer you are accustomed to say at night.

The examination of conscience is strongly recommended as a very important Christian duty, and is one of the most profitable and effectual means to avoid sin, and to acquire virtue; wherefore all persons who have at heart their salvation, and are truly desirous to please God, will constantly and diligently attend to the examination of conscience every night.

Prayer said in common, that is, by many together, is certainly more acceptable to God, and more beneficial, than prayer which is offered in private by one individual alone; and on this principle is chiefly grounded the pious and edifying practice in many families, of joining together in prayer every night; and it is most earnestly to be wished, that every Catholic family did adopt it.

The many signal blessings which God has bestowed on those families in which prayers are regularly said in common, should engage every head of a family to introduce and establish so laudable a custom; particularly at night, when all in the family may be assembled with greater convenience. "Where there are two or three gathered together in my name," says Christ, "there am I in the midst of them."[164]

---

[164] Mt 18:20

A Prayer to Our Angel Guardian

O holy angel! to whose care God, in his mercy, hath committed me; thou who assistest me in my wants, who consolest me in my afflictions, who supportest me when dejected, and who constantly obtainest for me new favors; I return thee now most sincere and humble thanks: and I conjure thee, O amiable guide! to continue still thy care; to defend me against my enemies; to remove from me the occasions of sin, to obtain for me a docility to thy holy inspirations; to protect me, in particular, at the hour of my death; and then conduct me to the mansions of eternal repose. Amen.

THE
CATECHISM

ORDERED BY THE

NATIONAL SYNOD OF MAYNOOTH

AND APPROVED OF BY

THE CARDINAL, THE ARCHBISHOPS, AND THE BISHOPS OF IRELAND

For general use throughout the Irish Church.

Imprimatur :

✠ EDUARDUS CARD. MACCABE,
ARCHIEPISCOPUS DUBLINENSIS,
HIBERNIÆ PRIMAS.

DUBLIN
M. H. GILL AND SON
50 UPPER SACKVILLE STREET
1884

Original Title Page

THE

Catechism

ORDERED BY THE

NATIONAL SYNOD OF MAYNOOTH

AND APPROVED OF BY

THE CARDINAL, THE ARCHBISHOPS, AND THE BISHOPS OF IRELAND

For general use through the Irish Church.

Imprimatur:

✠ Edwardus Card. MacCabe
Archiepiscopus Dublinensis,
Hiberniae Primas.

Copyright

DUBLIN

M. H. GILL AND SON

50 UPPER SACKVILLE STREET

1884

"And he went down with them, and came to Nazareth, and was subject to them." (Lk 2:51)

Introductory Prayers

In the name of the Father, and of the Son, and of the Holy Ghost.
Amen.

+

The Lord's Prayer

Our Father, who art in heaven, hallowed be thy name. Thy kingdom come; thy will be done on earth as it is in heaven. Give us this day our daily bread; and forgive us our trespasses, as we forgive them who trespass against us; and lead us not into temptation, but deliver us from evil. Amen.

The Angelical Salutation

Hail, Mary! full of grace, the Lord is with thee; blessed art thou among women, and blessed is the fruit of thy womb, Jesus. Holy Mary! Mother of God, pray for us, sinners, now, and at the hour of our death. Amen.

The Apostles' Creed

I believe in God, the Father Almighty, Creator of heaven and earth, and in Jesus Christ, his only Son, our Lord, who was conceived by the Holy Ghost, born of the Virgin Mary; suffered under Pontius Pilate; was crucified, dead, and buried; he descended into hell; the third day he rose again from the dead; he ascended into heaven, and sitteth at the right hand of God, the Father Almighty; from thence he shall come to judge the living and the dead. I believe in the Holy Ghost, the holy Catholic Church, the communion of saints, the forgiveness of sins, the resurrection of the body, life everlasting. Amen.

The Confiteor

I confess to Almighty God, to Blessed Mary ever Virgin, to blessed Michael the archangel, to blessed John the Baptist, to the holy apostles Peter and Paul, and to all the saints, that I have sinned exceedingly in thought, word, and deed, through my fault, through my fault, through my most grievous fault. Therefore I beseech the Blessed Mary ever Virgin, the blessed Michael the archangel, the blessed John the Baptist, the holy apostles Peter and Paul, and all the saints, to pray to the Lord our God for me.
May the Almighty God have mercy on me, forgive me my sins, and bring me to life everlasting. Amen.
May the Almighty and merciful Lord grant me pardon, absolution, and remission of my sins. Amen.

Indulgenced Prayers

Jesus, Mary, and Joseph, I offer you my heart and soul.
Jesus, Mary, and Joseph, assist me in my last agony.
Jesus, Mary, and Joseph, may I breathe forth my soul in peace with you.
(300 days indulgence.)

Let us pray.
O God! who in thine ineffable providence didst vouchsafe to choose blessed Joseph to be the spouse of thy most holy Mother, grant, we beseech thee, that we may be made worthy to receive him for our intercessor in heaven, whom we venerate as our holy and most powerful protector, who livest and reignest, world without end. Amen.

Grace before Meals

Bless us, O Lord, and these thy gifts which of thy bounty we are about to receive, through Christ our Lord. Amen.

Grace after Meals

We give thee thanks, O Almighty God, for all thy benefits; who livest and reignest, world without end. Amen.

May the souls of the faithful departed, through the mercy of God, rest in peace. Amen.

Prayers to Be Said Previous to Teaching Catechism

In the name of the Father, and of the Son, and of the Holy Ghost. Amen.

Anthem: Come, O Holy Ghost, replenish the hearts of thy faithful, and enkindle in them the fire of thy love.

V: Send forth thy Spirit, and they shall be created.

R: And thou shall renew the face of the earth.

Prayer: O Lord God of infinite bounty and mercy, grant us, we beseech thee, the grace to be always directed and comforted by thy Holy Spirit through Jesus Christ. Amen.

Direct, we beseech thee, O Lord, our actions by thy inspirations, and carry them on by thy assistance; that every prayer, instruction, and other work of ours may begin always from thee, and by thee be happily ended, through Christ our Lord. Amen.

Prayer after Teaching Catechism

Grant us, we beseech thee, O Lord, the help of thy grace, that what by thy instructions we know is to be done, by thy assistance we may perfectly accomplish, through Jesus Christ our Lord. Amen.

Acts of Contrition, Faith, Hope, and Charity

Let us pray.
O Almighty and eternal God, grant unto us an increase of faith, hope, and charity; and that we may obtain what thou hast promised, make us to love and practice what thou commandest, through Jesus Christ our Lord. Amen.

An Act of Contrition

O my God! I am heartily sorry for having offended thee, and I detest my sins above every other evil, because they displease thee, my God, who for thy infinite goodness art so deserving of all my love; and I firmly resolve, by thy holy grace, never more to offend thee, and to amend my life.

Short Act of Contrition

O my God, I am heartily sorry for my sins, and I detest them because they offend thee, who art so good, and I firmly resolve, with the help of thy holy grace, never again to commit sin.

An Act of Faith

O my God! I firmly believe that thou art one only God, the Creator and sovereign Lord of heaven and earth, infinitely great and infinitely good. I firmly believe that in thee, one only God, there are three divine Persons, really distinct, and equal in all things—the Father, and the Son, and the

Holy Ghost. I firmly believe that God the Son, the second Person of the most Holy Trinity, became man; that he was conceived by the Holy Ghost and was born of the Virgin Mary; that he suffered and died on a cross to redeem and save us; that he arose the third day from the dead; that he ascended into heaven; that he will come at the end of the world to judge mankind; that he will reward the good with eternal happiness, and condemn the wicked to the everlasting pains of hell. I believe these and all other articles which the holy Roman Catholic Church proposes to our belief, because thou, my God, the infallible truth, hast revealed them; and thou hast commanded us to hear the Church, which is the pillar and the ground of truth.[1] In this faith I am firmly resolved, by thy holy grace, to live and die.

An Act of Hope

O my God! who hast graciously promised every blessing, even heaven itself, through Jesus Christ, to those who keep thy commandments; relying on thy infinite power, goodness, and mercy, and on thy sacred promise, to which thou art always faithful, I confidently hope to obtain pardon of all my sins, grace to serve thee faithfully in this life, by doing the good works thou hast commanded, and which, with thy assistance, I now purpose to perform, and eternal happiness in the next, through my Lord and Savior Jesus Christ.

An Act of Charity

O my God! I love thee with my whole heart and soul, and above all things, because thou art infinitely good and perfect, and most worthy of all my love; and for thy sake, I love my neighbor as myself. Mercifully grant, O my

---

[1] Cf. Mt 18:17; 1 Tm 3:15

God! that having loved thee on earth, I may love and enjoy thee forever in heaven. Amen.

A Prayer to Be Said before Mass

O merciful Father! who didst so love the world as to give up, for our re-demption thy beloved Son, who, in obedience to thee, and for us sinners, humbled himself unto the death of the cross, and continues to offer himself daily, by the ministry of his priests, for the living and the dead; we humbly beseech thee that, penetrated with a lively faith, we may always assist, with the utmost devotion and reverence, at the oblation of his most precious body and blood, which is made at Mass, and thereby be made partakers of the sacrifice which he consummated on Calvary.

In union with the holy Church and its ministers, and invoking the Blessed Virgin Mary, Mother of God, with all the angels and saints, we now offer the adorable Sacrifice of the Mass to thy honor and glory, to acknowledge thy infinite perfections, thy supreme dominion over all thy creatures, our entire subjection to thee, and total dependence on thy gra-cious providence, and in thanksgiving for all thy benefits, and for the remission of our sins.

We offer it for the propagation of the Catholic faith, for our most holy father the pope, for our bishop, and for all the pastors and clergy of thy holy Church, that they may direct the faithful in the way of salvation; for all that are in high station, that we may lead quiet and holy lives; for peace and goodwill among all states and peoples, for the necessities of mankind, and particularly for the congregation here present, to obtain all blessings we stand in need of in this life, everlasting happiness in the next, and eternal rest to the faithful departed.

And as Jesus Christ so ordained, when he instituted at his last supper this wonderful mystery of his power, wisdom, and goodness, we offer the Mass in grateful remembrance of all he has done and suffered for the love of us, making special commemoration of his bitter passion and death, and of his glorious resurrection and ascension into heaven.

Vouchsafe, O Almighty and eternal God (for to thee alone the homage of sacrifice is due), graciously to accept it for these and all other purposes agreeable to thy holy will; and to render it the more pleasing, we offer it to thee, through the same Jesus Christ, thy beloved Son, our Lord and Savior, our high priest and victim, and in the name of the most Holy Trinity, the Father, and the Son, and the Holy Ghost, to whom be honor, praise and glory, forever and ever. Amen.

The Angelus

1. The angel of the Lord declared unto Mary:
And she conceived of the Holy Ghost.
Hail Mary! full of grace, the Lord is with thee; blessed art thou among women, and blessed is the fruit of thy womb, Jesus. Holy Mary! Mother of God, pray for us, sinners, now, and at the hour of our death. Amen.
2. Behold the handmaid of the Lord:
Be it done unto me according to thy word.
Hail Mary and Holy Mary.
3. And the Word was made flesh:
And dwelt among us.
Hail Mary and Holy Mary.
Pray for us, O holy Mother of God.
That we may be made worthy of the promises of Christ.

Let us pray.
Pour forth, we beseech thee, O Lord, thy grace into our hearts, that we, to whom the incarnation of Christ, thy Son, was made known by the message of an angel, may, by his passion and cross, be brought to the glory of his resurrection, through the same Christ our Lord. Amen.

May the divine assistance always remain with us.
And may the souls of the faithful departed, through the mercy of God, rest in peace. Amen.

Chapter 1

LESSON 1

On God and the Creation of the World

1. **Who made the world?**

   God made the world.

2. **Who is God?**

   God is the Creator and sovereign Lord of heaven and earth and of all things.

3. **How many gods are there?**

   There is but one God, who will reward the good and punish the wicked.

4. **Where is God?**

   God is everywhere; but he manifests his glory in heaven, where he is enjoyed by the blessed.

5. **What is heaven?**

Heaven is the kingdom of God's glory, and of his angels and saints.

6. **If God be everywhere, why do we not see him?**

We do not see God, because he is a pure spirit, having no body, and therefore cannot be seen by us in this life.

7. **Does God see us?**

God sees us and continually watches over us.

8. **Does God know all things?**

God knows all things, even our most secret thoughts and actions; "all things are naked and open to his eyes."[2]

9. **Will God judge our most secret thoughts and actions?**

God will judge our most secret thoughts and actions; and "every idle word that men shall speak, they shall render an account for it in the day of judgment."[3]

10. **Had God a beginning?**

God had no beginning; he always was, and always will be.

11. **Can God do all things?**

God can do all things; for "with God all things are possible," and nothing is difficult to him.[4]

12. **How did God make the world?**

God made the world from nothing; and by his word only—that is, by a single act of his all-powerful will.

---

[2] Heb 4:13
[3] Mt 12:36
[4] Mt 19:26

13. **Why did God make the world?**

God made the world for his own glory, to show his power and wisdom, and for man's use and benefit.[5]

LESSON 2

On Man and the End of His Creation

14. **What is man?**

Man is one of God's creatures, composed of a body and soul, and made unto God's likeness.

15. **In what is man made to God's likeness?**

Man is made to God's likeness in his soul.

16. **In what is man's soul like to God?**

Man's soul is like to God in being a spirit and immortal, and in being capable of knowing and loving God.

17. **What do you mean when you say the soul is immortal?**

By saying the soul is immortal, I mean that it can never die.

18. **For what end did God make us?**

God made us to know, love, and serve him here on earth; and to see and enjoy him forever in heaven.

19. **How can we know God on earth?**

We can know God on earth by learning the truths he has taught.

20. **Where shall we find the truths God has taught?**

The truths God has taught are chiefly contained in the Apostles' Creed.

[5] Cf. Ps 18

LESSON 3

On the Apostles' Creed

21. What does the Apostles' Creed contain?

The Apostles' Creed contains the principal mysteries of religion, and other necessary articles.

22. Which are the principal mysteries of religion?

The principal mysteries of religion are the unity and trinity of God, the incarnation, death, and resurrection of our Savior—which are most necessary to be known and believed.

23. What do you mean by mysteries of religion?

Mysteries of religion are revealed truths which we cannot comprehend.

24. Why does God require of us to believe mysteries of religion?

God requires of us to believe mysteries that we may pay him the homage of our understanding.

25. How do we pay the homage of our understanding to God?

We pay the homage of our understanding to God, by firmly believing on God's word whatever he has revealed, be it ever so difficult to us.

26. Must we also submit our will to God?

We must submit our will to God by cheerfully doing, in obedience to God, all things whatsoever he commands.

27. What means the unity of God?

The unity of God means there is but one God, and there cannot be more gods than one.[6]

---

[6] Cf. Eph 4:6

28. **Why cannot there be more gods than one?**

There cannot be more gods than one, because God being supreme and infinite, cannot have an equal.

LESSON 4

On the Trinity and Incarnation

29. **How many Persons are there in God?**

In God there are three divine Persons, really distinct and equal in all things: the Father, the Son, and the Holy Ghost.

30. **Is the Father God?**

The Father is God, and the first Person of the Blessed Trinity.

31. **Is the Son God?**

The Son is God, and the second Person of the Blessed Trinity.

32. **Is the Holy Ghost God?**

The Holy Ghost is God, and the third Person of the Blessed Trinity.

33. **What means the Blessed Trinity?**

The Blessed Trinity means one God in three divine Persons.

34. **Are the three divine Persons three gods?**

The three divine Persons are one only God, having but one and the same divine nature, and they are from eternity.

35. **Is any one of the three divine Persons more powerful or wiser than another?**

No one of the three divine Persons can be more powerful or wiser than another, because the three divine Persons are all one and the same God, and therefore they must be alike in all divine perfections.

36. Did one of the divine Persons become man?

God the Son, the second divine Person, became man.[7]

37. How did God the Son become man?

God the Son became man by taking a body and soul like ours in the chaste womb of the Virgin Mary by the power and operation of the Holy Ghost.

THE ANNUNCIATION

38. How do you call God the Son made man?

God the Son made man is called Jesus Christ.

[7] Cf. Jn 1:14

39. **What is the meaning of the words *Jesus Christ?***

Jesus signifies *Savior*; and Christ signifies *the anointed*; and St. Paul says, that "in the name of Jesus every knee should bend."[8]

40. **Did Jesus remain God when he became man?**

Jesus Christ remains always God.

41. **Was Jesus Christ always man?**

Jesus Christ was man only from the time of his conception or incarnation.

42. **What means the incarnation?**

The incarnation means that God the Son, the second Person of the Blessed Trinity, was made man.[9]

43. **What do you believe Jesus Christ to be?**

I believe Jesus Christ to be true God and true man.

44. **Why did God the Son become man?**

God the Son became man to redeem and save us.

45. **How did Christ redeem and save us?**

Christ redeemed and saved us by his sufferings and death on the cross.

46. **Was it by his passion and death also Christ satisfied the justice of God for our sins?**

By his passion and death Christ satisfied the justice of God, and delivered us from hell, and from the power of the devil.

[8] Phil 2:10
[9] Cf. Jn 1:14

Chapter 2

LESSON 5

On Our First Parents, Etc.

47. **How came we to be in the power of the devil?**
We came to be in the power of the devil by the disobedience of our first parents in eating the forbidden fruit.[10]

48. **Who were our first parents?**
Our first parents were Adam and Eve, the first man and woman.

49. **Why did God command our first parents not to eat the forbidden fruit?**
God commanded our first parents not to eat the forbidden fruit in order to prove to them his dominion over them, and their dependence on him—and to try their obedience.

50. **Who tempted our first parents to eat the forbidden fruit?**
The devil, envying our first parents their happy state, tempted them to eat the forbidden fruit.[11]

51. **Whom do you mean by the devil?**
By the devil I mean one of the rebellious or fallen angels whom God cast out of heaven.

52. **What do you mean by angels?**
Angels are pure spirits without a body, created to adore and enjoy God in heaven.

[10] Cf. Gn 2-3
[11] Cf. Gn 3

53. **Were the angels created for any other purpose?**

The angels were also created to assist before the throne of God, and to minister unto him; they have been often sent as messengers from God to man, and are also appointed our guardians.[12]

54. **Why were any of the angels cast out of heaven?**

Some of the angels were cast out of heaven because through pride they rebelled against God.[13]

55. **Did God punish in any other way the angels who rebelled?**

God condemned the rebellious angels to hell—a place of eternal torments.

56. **Why did God make hell?**

God made hell to punish the devils or bad angels.

57. **Are any others condemned to hell besides the devils or bad angels?**

Besides the devils or bad angels all are condemned to hell who die enemies to God, that is, all who die in a state of mortal sin.

58. **Can anyone come out of hell?**

No one can come out of hell, for out of hell there is no redemption.

59. **How did God reward the angels who remained faithful?**

God rewarded the angels who remained faithful by confirming them forever in glory.

[12] Cf. Apoc 7:11; Heb 1:7; Mt 4:11; 18:10
[13] Cf. Is 14:11-15

LESSON 6

On Original Sin, Etc.

60. **What evil effects followed the disobedience of our first parents?**
    Our first parents by their disobedience lost their original justice and all right to heaven. They were driven out of the garden of paradise, and condemned to death with their posterity.

61. **What were the chief blessings intended for our first parents, had they remained faithful to God?**
    The chief blessings intended for our first parents if they remained faithful, were a constant state of happiness in this life and eternal glory in the next.

62. **What evils befell us in consequence of the disobedience of our first parents?**
    We were all made partakers of the sin and punishment of our first parents, as we should be all sharers in their innocence and happiness, if they had been obedient to God.[14]

63. **What other particular effects follow from the sin of our first parents?**
    Our whole nature was corrupted by the sin of our first parents—it darkened our understanding, weakened our will, and left in us a strong inclination to evil.

64. **What is original sin?**
    Original sin is the sin we inherit from our first parents, and in which we were conceived and born "children of wrath."[15]

65. **Why is original sin so called?**
    Original sin is so called because it is transmitted to us from our first parents—and we came into the world infected with it.

---

[14] Cf. Rom 5:12
[15] Eph 2:3

66. **Does this corruption of nature remain in us after original sin is forgiven?**

This corruption of nature and many other temporal punishments remain after original sin is forgiven, and serve for our trial and an occasion of merit.

67. **Has original sin been transmitted to all the descendants of our first parents without exception?**

The Blessed Virgin Mary, by a singular privilege of grace, bestowed on her through the merits of her divine Son, was preserved free from the guilt of original sin, and this privilege is called her immaculate conception.

LESSON 7

On Jesus Christ, Etc.

68. **Did God the Son become man immediately after the transgression of our first parents?**

God the Son did not become man immediately after the sin of our first parents, though he was immediately promised to them as a Redeemer.[16]

69. **How many years after the fall of our first parents did God the Son become man?**

God the Son became man about four thousand years after the fall of our first parents.

70. **How could they be saved who lived before God the Son became man?**

They who lived before God the Son became man could be saved by the belief of a Redeemer to come, and by keeping the commandments of God.

[16] Cf. Gn 3:15

71. **On what day did God the Son become man?**

God the Son became man on the twenty-fifth of March, the day of the annunciation.

72. **Why is it called the day of the annunciation?**

The day of the annunciation is so called because on that day the Angel Gabriel announced to the Virgin Mary: "Behold, thou shalt conceive in thy womb, and shalt bring forth a son, and thou shalt call his name Jesus."[17]

73. **On what day was Christ born of the Virgin Mary?**

Christ was born on Christmas day, in a stable at Bethlehem.

THE NATIVITY

---

[17] Lk 1:31

74. **How long did Christ live on earth?**

Christ lived on earth about thirty-three years, and led a most holy life in poverty and sufferings.

75. **Why did Christ live so long on earth?**

Christ lived so long upon earth to show us the way to heaven, by his instructions and example.

76. **How did Christ end his life?**

On Good Friday, Christ was crucified on Mount Calvary, and died nailed to a cross.

77. **Why do you call that day good on which Christ suffered so painful and ignominious a death?**

We call that day good on which Christ died because by his death on the cross he showed the excess of his love, and purchased every blessing for us.

78. **Who condemned Christ to so cruel a death?**

Pontius Pilate, the Roman governor, condemned Christ to death at the desire of the Jews.

79. **What lesson do we learn from the sufferings and death of Christ?**

From the sufferings and death of Christ we learn the enormity of sin, the hatred God bears to it, and the necessity of satisfying for it.

80. **Did anything remarkable happen at the death of Christ?**

At the death of Christ the sun was darkened, the earth trembled, and the dead arose, and appeared to many.[18]

---

[18] Cf. Mt 27:45-53

LESSON 8

On Christ's Descent into Hell, and on His Resurrection and Ascension into Heaven

81. **Where did Christ's soul go after his death?**

After Christ's death his soul descended into hell.

82. **Did Christ's soul descend into the hell of the damned?**

The hell into which Christ's soul descended was not the hell of the damned, but a place or state of rest called limbo, where the souls of the saints who died before Christ were damned.

83. **Why did Christ's soul descend into limbo?**

Christ descended into limbo, St. Peter says, "to preach to those souls who were in prison," that is, to announce to them in person the joyful tidings of their redemption.[19]

84. **Why did not the souls of saints go to heaven immediately after their death?**

Heaven was shut against mankind by the sin of our first parents, and it could not be opened to anyone but by the death of Christ.

85. **When did the souls of the saints who died before Christ go to heaven?**

The souls of the saints who died before Christ went to heaven when Christ ascended into heaven.

86. **Where was Christ's body while his soul was in limbo?**

When Christ's soul was in limbo his body was in the sepulcher or grave.

87. **On what day did Christ rise from the dead?**

On Easter Sunday, the third day after his death, Christ arose in body and soul, glorious and immortal from the dead.

[19] 1 Pt 3:19

88. **What do the death and resurrection of Christ prove?**
By dying on the cross Christ showed himself a real mortal man, and by raising himself from the dead, he proved himself God.

89. **How long did Christ stay on earth after his resurrection?**
Christ stayed on earth forty days after his resurrection, to show that he was truly risen from the dead, and to instruct his apostles.

90. **After Christ had remained forty days on earth, where did he go?**
After forty days, Christ, on Ascension day, ascended from Mount Olivet, with his body and soul, into heaven.

91. **Where is Christ in heaven?**
Christ sits at the right hand of God the Father Almighty, in heaven.

92. **What do you mean by saying that Christ sits at the right hand of God?**
When I say Christ sits at the right hand of God, I mean that Christ as God is equal to his Father in all things, and that as man he is in the highest place in heaven, next to God in power and glory.

93. **Did Christ make any special promise to his apostles before he ascended into heaven?**
Before he ascended into heaven, Christ promised to his apostles that he would send the Holy Ghost, the Spirit of truth, to teach them all things, and to abide with them forever.[20]

---

[20] Cf. Jn 14:16-17; 15:26; 16:13

Chapter 3

LESSON 9

On the Descent of the Holy Ghost, on the New Law, and on the Sign of the Cross

94. **On what day, and after what manner, did the Holy Ghost descend on the apostles?**

On Whitsunday, the Holy Ghost descended on the apostles in the form of tongues of fire.[21]

95. **What does the scripture say of those who received the Holy Ghost?**

The scripture says: "They were all filled with the Holy Ghost, and they began to speak in diverse tongues...the wonderful works of God."[22]

96. **Why did Christ send the Holy Ghost?**

Christ sent the Holy Ghost to sanctify his Church, to comfort his apostles, and to enable them to preach his gospel, or the new law.

97. **What do you mean by the new law?**

The new law is that which Christ established on earth.

98. **Which was the old law?**

The old law was that given to the Jews.

99. **How do you call the followers of the new law?**

The followers of the new law are called Christians.

---

[21] Cf. Acts 2:1-4
[22] Acts 2:4, 11

100. **How are we known to be Christians?**

We are known to be Christians by being baptized, by professing the doctrine of Christ, and by the sign of the cross.

101. **How is the sign of the cross made?**

The sign of the cross is made by putting the right hand to the forehead, then under the breast, then to the left and right shoulders, saying: "In the name of the Father, and of the Son, and of the Holy Ghost. Amen."

102. **Why do we make the sign of the cross?**

We make the sign of the cross to beg that Jesus Christ, by his cross and passion, may bless and protect us.

103. **Should we frequently make the sign of the cross?**

We should frequently make the sign of the cross, particularly in all temptations and dangers, and before and after prayer, but we should always make it with great attention and devotion.

104. **What does the sign of the cross signify?**

The sign of the cross signifies, and brings to our minds, the mysteries of the Blessed Trinity and the incarnation and death of our Savior.

105. **How does the sign of the cross remind us of the Blessed Trinity?**

The sign of the cross reminds us of the Blessed Trinity, because, in making the sign of the cross we invoke the three divine Persons, saying: "In the name of the Father, and of the Son, and of the Holy Ghost."

106. **How does the sign of the cross bring to our mind the incarnation and death of our Savior?**

The sign of the cross brings to our mind the incarnation and death of our Savior, because, as he suffered death in human flesh on a cross, the sign of the cross must naturally remind all true Christians of his incarnation and death.

107. **Where are true Christians to be found?**

True Christians are to be found only in the true Church.

LESSON 10

On the True Church

108. **What do you mean by the true Church?**

The true Church is the congregation of all the faithful, who, being baptized, profess the same faith, partake of the same sacraments, and are governed by their lawful pastors, under one visible head on earth.

109. **How do you call the true Church?**

The true Church is called the holy Catholic Church.

110. **Is there any other true Church besides the holy Catholic Church?**

As there is but "one Lord, one faith, one baptism, one God and Father of all," there can be but the one true Church.[23]

111. **Are all obliged to be of the true Church?**

All are obliged to belong to the true Church, and no one can be saved out of it.[24]

112. **Will strict honesty towards everyone, and moral good works, ensure salvation, whatever religion one professes?**

Strict honesty and moral good works will not ensure salvation unless they be enlivened by "faith that worketh by charity."[25]

113. **Why must our good works be enlivened by faith?**

Our good works must be enlivened by faith, because the scripture says:

[23] Eph 4:5-6
[24] Cf. Acts 2; Lk 10; Jn 10; Mt 18
[25] Gal 5:6

"Without faith it is impossible to please God," and "he that believeth not shall be condemned."[26]

114. **Are we justified by faith alone without good works?**

We are not justified by faith alone without good works; "for as the body without the spirit is dead, so also faith without works is dead."[27]

115. **Must our good works be also enlivened by charity?**

Our good works must be enlivened by charity; for St. Paul says: "If I should distribute all my goods to feed the poor, and if I should deliver my body to be burned, and have not charity, it profiteth me nothing."[28]

116. **What is that charity of which St. Paul speaks?**

The charity of which St. Paul speaks is that pure and sincere love of God which makes us do his will in all things, and be obedient to his Church, which he commands us to hear.[29]

117. **Which are the marks of the true Church?**

The marks of the true Church are that it is one, holy, Catholic, and apostolical.

118. **How is the Church one?**

The Church is one in being "one body" animated by "one spirit," and one fold under one head and shepherd, Jesus Christ, who is over all the Church.[30]

119. **In what else is the Church one?**

The Church is also one, in all its members believing the same truths,

---

[26] Heb 11:6; Mk 16:16
[27] Jas 2:26
[28] 1 Cor 13:3
[29] Cf. Mt 18:17; Lk 10:16
[30] Cf. Eph 4:4

having the same sacraments and sacrifice, and being under one visible head on earth.

120. **How is the Church holy?**

The Church is holy in its founder, Jesus Christ, in its doctrines, sacraments, and sacrifice, and in the number of its children who have been eminent for holiness in all ages.

121. **How is the Church catholic or universal?**

The Church is catholic or universal, because it has subsisted in every age, is spread throughout all nations, and shall last to the end of time.[31]

THE AGONY IN THE GARDEN

---

[31] Cf. Mt 28:18-20; Rom 10

122. How is the Church apostolical?

The Church is apostolical, because it was founded by Christ on his apostles, and is governed by their lawful successors, and because it never ceased, and never will cease, to teach their doctrine.[32]

LESSON 11

The Church Continued

123. Why do you call the Church Roman?

The Church is called Roman, because the visible head of the Church is the bishop of Rome.

124. Who is the visible head of the Church?

The pope, who is Christ's vicar on earth, is visible head of the Church.

125. To whom does the pope succeed as visible head of the Church?

The pope succeeds to St. Peter, who was chief of the apostles, Christ's vicar on earth and first pope and bishop of Rome.

126. How does it appear that St. Peter was made head of the Church?

Christ said to St. Peter: "Thou art Peter, and upon this rock I will build my church...and I will give to thee the keys of the kingdom of heaven."[33] And again: "Feed my lambs...feed my sheep."[34]

127. What do these texts of scripture prove?

These texts of scripture prove that Christ committed to St. Peter, and to his lawful successors, the care of his whole flock, that is, of his whole Church, both pastors and people.

[32] Cf. Eph 2:20
[33] Mt 16:18-19
[34] Jn 21:15-17

128. **Who succeeded to the other apostles?**

The successors of the other apostles are the bishops of the holy Catholic Church.

129. **By whom was Ireland converted to the true faith?**

Ireland was converted to the true faith by St. Patrick, who was sent by Pope Celestine, and came to our island in the year 432.

130. **Can the Church err in what it teaches?**

The Church cannot err in what it teaches; because, Christ said to the pastors of his Church: "Go ye, therefore, teach all nations...and behold I am with you all days even to the end of the world."[35]

131. **Can the pope err in what he teaches?**

The pope can no more err than the Church, when, as supreme pastor, he teaches doctrines of faith or morals, to be held by all the faithful.

132. **For what purpose does Christ remain with his Church?**

Christ remains always with his Church, that he himself, directing and assisting by his Holy Spirit the pastors of his Church, may teach all ages, and all nations.

133. **What else did Christ promise to his Church?**

Christ also promised to his Church that "the gates of hell shall not prevail against it."[36]

134. **What other advantages have we in the true Church?**

In the true Church, besides the true faith, we have the communion of saints and the forgiveness of sins.

---

[35] Mt 28:19-20
[36] Mt 16:18

135. **What means the forgiveness of sins?**

The forgiveness of sins means, that Christ left to the pastors of his Church the power of forgiving sins.[37]

Chapter 4

LESSON 12

On Sin

136. **What is sin?**

Sin is any willful thought, word, deed, or omission contrary to the law of God.

137. **What is mortal sin?**

Mortal sin is a grievous offense or transgression against the law of God.

138. **Why is it called mortal?**

Mortal sin is so called, because it kills the soul by depriving it of its true life, which is sanctifying grace, and because it brings everlasting death and damnation to the soul.

139. **What is venial sin?**

Venial sin is a less grievous offense or transgression against the law of God.

140. **Does venial sin deprive the soul of sanctifying grace, and deserve everlasting punishment?**

Venial sin does not deprive the soul of sanctifying grace, or deserve everlasting punishment, but it hurts the soul by lessening its love for God, and

---

[37] Cf. Jn 20:23

disposing it to mortal sin. The scripture says, "He that contemneth small things shall fall by little and little."[38]

141. What is grace?

Grace is a supernatural gift bestowed on us by God for our salvation.

142. What is sanctifying grace?

Sanctifying grace is that grace which makes the soul holy and pleasing to God.

143. What is actual grace?

Actual grace is that which helps us to do good works, and to avoid sin.

144. Is grace necessary to salvation?

Without grace we can do nothing to merit heaven, and "without me," says Christ, "you can do nothing."[39]

145. Is it a great misfortune to fall into mortal sin?

To fall into mortal sin is the greatest of all misfortunes.

146. What must we do if we fall into mortal sin?

If we fall into mortal sin we ought to repent sincerely, and go to confession as soon as we can.

147. Why should we go to confession as soon as we can after falling into mortal sin?

We ought to go to confession as soon as we can after falling into mortal sin, that we may recover God's friendship and be always prepared to die.

[38] Ecclus 19:1
[39] Jn 15:5

148. **What should we do if we cannot go to confession soon after falling into mortal sin?**

If we cannot go to confession soon after falling into mortal sin, we ought to excite ourselves to perfect contrition, with the intention of going to confession.

149. **How do you express an act of perfect contrition?**

O my God! I am heartily sorry for having offended thee, and I detest my sins above every other evil, because they displease thee, my God, who for thy infinite goodness art so deserving of all my love; and I firmly resolve, by thy holy grace, never more to offend thee, and to amend my life.

150. **Will perfect contrition reconcile us to God?**

Perfect contrition will reconcile us to God, and give us pardon of our sins.

151. **What is necessary for our contrition to be perfect?**

That our contrition may be perfect, we should be heartily sorry for our sins, and detest them above every other evil, because they offend God, who is so good in himself, with a firm resolution not to offend God anymore, to satisfy for our sins, and to go to confession.

152. **What are the sins that are called capital sins?**

There are seven kinds of sin that are called capital sins—pride, covetousness, lust, anger, gluttony, envy, and sloth.

153. **Where do they go who die in mortal sin?**

They who die in mortal sin go to hell, for all eternity.

154. **Where do they go who have not done penance for their venial sins?**

They who die without doing penance for their venial sins go to purgatory.

LESSON 13

On Purgatory

155. **What is purgatory?**

Purgatory is a place or state of punishment in the next life where some souls suffer for a time before they go to heaven.[40]

156. **Do any others go to purgatory besides those who die in venial sin?**

Besides those who die in venial sin, those also go to purgatory who die indebted to God's justice on account of mortal sin.

157. **When God forgives mortal sin, as to its guilt, and the eternal punishment it deserves, does he require temporary punishment to be suffered for it?**

When God forgives mortal sin, he very often requires some temporary punishment to be suffered for it, that we may be deterred from relapsing into sin, and that we may make some atonement to his offended majesty and goodness.[41]

158. **Can the souls in purgatory be relieved by our prayers and other good works?**

As the souls in purgatory are children of God, and still members of the Church, they share in the communion of saints, and are relieved by our prayers and other good works; for the scripture says, "It is a holy and a wholesome thought to pray for the dead that they may be loosed from their sins."[42]

159. **What does the communion of saints mean?**

The communion of saints is the union that exists between the members of the true Church on earth with each other, and with the blessed in heaven, and the suffering souls in purgatory.

[40] Cf. Mt 12:32
[41] Cf. Nm 14; 2 Kgs 12
[42] 2 Mc 12:46

160. **What benefits follow from the communion of saints?**

Through the communion of saints, the faithful on earth assist each other by their prayers and good works, and are aided by the intercession of the saints in heaven, while both the saints in heaven and the faithful on earth help the souls in purgatory.

161. **Is it sufficient for salvation to be members of the true Church?**

It is not sufficient for salvation to be members of the true Church; we must "avoid evil and do good."[43]

162. **"What good shall I do that I may have life everlasting?"[44]**

"If thou wilt enter into life," says Christ, "keep the commandments."[45]

163. **What commandments am I to keep?**

I am to keep the ten commandments of God.

Chapter 5

LESSON 14

On the Ten Commandments

164. **Say the ten commandments of God.**

The ten commandments of God are:

1. I am the Lord thy God; thou shalt not have strange gods before me.
2. Thou shalt not take the name of the Lord thy God in vain.
3. Remember that thou keep holy the sabbath-day.
4. Honor thy father and thy mother.

---

[43] 1 Pt 3:11
[44] Mt 19:16
[45] Mt 19:17

5. Thou shalt not kill.

6. Thou shalt not commit adultery.

7. Thou shalt not steal.

8. Thou shalt not bear false witness against thy neighbor.

9. Thou shalt not covet thy neighbor's wife.

10. Thou shalt not covet thy neighbor's goods.[46]

165. **Is it necessary to keep all and every one of the ten commandments?**

It is necessary to keep every one of the ten commandments; for the scripture says, whosoever shall offend in one shall become guilty of all.[47]

166. **Say the first commandment.**

The first commandment is: I am the Lord thy God; thou shalt not have strange gods before me.

167. **What is commanded by the first commandment?**

We are commanded by the first commandment to adore one God, and to adore him alone.

168. **How are we to adore God?**

We are to adore God by faith, hope, and charity, by prayer and sacrifice.

169. **What is faith?**

Faith is a divine virtue, by which we firmly believe the truths which God has revealed.

170. **How do we know with certainty what God has revealed?**

We know with certainty what God has revealed by the authority of his Church, which is "the pillar and the ground of truth."[48]

[46] Cf. Ex 20
[47] Cf. Jas 2:10
[48] 1 Tm 3:15

THE SCOURGING OF JESUS

171. **Why do we believe what God teaches?**

We believe what God teaches because he is the infallible truth, and therefore cannot deceive nor be deceived.

172. **What is hope?**

Hope is a divine virtue, by which we desire and firmly expect that God will give us eternal life, and the means to obtain it.

173. **Why do we hope in God?**

We hope in God because he is infinitely powerful, good, and merciful, and because he is faithful to his word and has promised all graces, even heaven itself, through Jesus Christ to all those who keep his commandments.

174. What is charity?

Charity is a divine virtue, by which we love God above all for his own sake, and our neighbor as ourselves for the love of God.

175. Why should we love God above all for his own sake?

We should love God above all for his own sake, because God alone is infinitely good and perfect.

176. How are we to love God above all?

We are to love God above all, by loving him more than ourselves, and more than anything in the world, and by being disposed to sacrifice everything that is most dear to us, even life, if necessary, rather than offend him by mortal sin.

177. Should we frequently make acts of faith, hope, and charity?

We should frequently make acts of faith, hope, and charity, particularly when we come to the use of reason, and at the hour of death, and also when we are tempted to sin against any of those divine virtues, or have sinned against them.

LESSON 15

On the First Commandment

178. What is forbidden by the first commandment?

The first commandment forbids all sins against faith, hope, and charity, and other duties of religion.

179. How does a person sin against faith?

A person sins against faith, by not endeavoring to know what God has taught, by not believing what God has taught, and by denying or not professing his belief in what God has taught.

180. **Who are they who do not endeavor to know what God has taught?**

They who do not endeavor to know what God has taught are those who neglect to learn the Christian doctrine.

181. **Who are they who do not believe what God has taught?**

They who do not believe what God has taught are the heretics and infidels.

182. **Who are they who sin against faith by denying what God has taught?**

All those sin against faith by denying what God has taught, who by any outward act, profession, or declaration, deny the true religion in which they inwardly believe.

183. **Can persons who deny outwardly the true religion in which they inwardly believe expect salvation while in that state?**

They who deny outwardly the true religion cannot expect salvation, for Christ has said: "Whosoever shall deny me before men, I will also deny him before my Father who is in heaven."[49]

184. **Are we obliged to make open profession of our faith or religion?**

We are obliged to make open profession of our faith or religion, as often as God's honor, our own spiritual good, or our neighbor's edification requires it—"Whosoever," says Christ, "shall confess me before men, I will also confess him before my Father who is in heaven."[50]

185. **Have you anything further to add regarding the profession of faith?**

He who believes in the true Church, and says that in his heart he is attached to it, but through pride, human respect, or worldly motives, disguises his religion, or does not comply with its essential duties, sins against the obligation of professing the true faith.

---

[49] Mt 10:33
[50] Mt 10:32

186. **What does St. Paul say of apostates, that is, of those who are "fallen away" from the true religion or Church?**[51]

St. Paul says of apostates, that "it is impossible for them...to be renewed again to penance," that is, their conversion is extremely difficult.[52]

187. **Why is the conversion of apostates so very difficult?**

The conversion of apostates is very difficult, because by their apostasy they sin against the Holy Ghost, "crucify again the Son of God, and make a mockery of him."[53]

188. **Which are the sins against hope?**

The sins against hope are despair and presumption.

189. **What is despair?**

Despair is the loss of confidence in God.

190. **What is presumption?**

Presumption is a foolish expectation of salvation, without making proper use of the necessary means to obtain it.

191. **How does a person sin against the love of God?**

A person sins against the love of God by every sin, but particularly by mortal sin.

192. **How does a person sin against the love of his neighbor?**

A person sins against the love of his neighbor by injuring him in any respect, and by not assisting him when able in his spiritual or corporal necessities.

---

[51] Cf. Heb 6:6
[52] Heb 6:4-6
[53] Heb 6:6

LESSON 16

The First Commandment Continued

193. **What else is forbidden by this first commandment?**

    The first commandment also forbids us to give to any creature the honor due to God alone.

194. **Are we forbidden to honor the saints?**

    We are not forbidden to honor the saints, if we only honor them as God's special friends and faithful servants, and if we do not give them supreme or divine honor, which belongs to God alone.

195. **Do Catholics distinguish between the honor they give to God and the honor they give to the saints, when they pray to God and the saints?**

    Catholics distinguish between the honor they give to God and the honor they give to the saints: for, of God alone they beg grace and mercy, and of the saints they only ask the assistance of their prayers.[54]

196. **Is it lawful to recommend ourselves to the saints, and to ask their prayers?**

    It is lawful to recommend ourselves to the saints, and to ask their prayers, as it is lawful, and a very pious practice, to ask the prayers of our fellow creatures on earth, and to pray for them.[55]

197. **Why do Catholics kneel before the images of Christ and his saints?**

    Catholics kneel before the images of Christ and his saints to honor Christ and his saints, whom their images represent.[56]

---

[54] Cf. Tb 12:12
[55] Cf. 1 Thes 5:25; Jas 5:16
[56] Cf. Ex 25:18

198. **Is it proper to show any mark of respect to the crucifix, and to the pictures of Christ and his saints?**

It is proper to show respect to the crucifix and religious pictures, because they represent Christ and his saints, and remind us of them.[57]

199. **Why do Catholics honor the relics of the saints?**

Catholics honor the relics of the saints, because their bodies were the temples of the Holy Ghost, and will be honored at the last day and will be glorified forever in heaven.

200. **Are we then to pray to the crucifix or to the images and relics of the saints?**

We are not to pray to the crucifix or to the images and relics of saints; for they have neither life, nor sense, nor power to hear or help us.

201. **Why, then, do we pray before the crucifix, and before the images and relics of the saints?**

We pray before the crucifix and before the relics of the saints because they are holy and excite our devotion, by reminding us of Christ and his saints, and they also encourage us to imitate their virtues and good works.[58]

202. **Is it not forbidden by the first commandment to make images?**

It is not forbidden to make images, if we do not make them for gods, to adore and serve them, as the idolators do.

203. **Is there anything else forbidden by the first commandment?**

The first commandment also forbids all dealings and communications with the devil, and the inquiring, by improper means, after things lost, hidden, or to come.

204. **Is it also forbidden to give credit to dreams and fortune-telling?**

It is forbidden to give credit to dreams and fortune-telling, and also all

---

[57] Cf. Acts 19:12; Mt 9:20-22
[58] Cf. Ex 25:18; Jn 3:14

incantations, charms and spells, and superstitious observances of omens and accidents are very sinful.

205. **What do you think of theatrical representations and other amusements, particularly at wakes, in which religion, its ministers, and sacred ceremonies are ridiculed?**

Theatrical representations and other amusements in which sacred things are ridiculed, and all such representations at wakes, are highly criminal, and are strictly forbidden by the first commandment.

Chapter 6

LESSON 17

On the Second, Third, and Fourth Commandments

206. **Say the second commandment.**

The second commandment is: Thou shalt not take the name of the Lord thy God in vain.

207. **What is commanded by the second commandment?**

We are commanded by the second commandment to speak with reverence of God, and of his saints and ministers of religion, its practices and ceremonies, and of all things relating to divine service.

208. **What else is commanded by the second commandment?**

We are also commanded, by the second commandment, to keep our lawful oaths and vows.

209. **What is forbidden by the second commandment?**

The second commandment forbids all oaths that are false, rash, unjust, and unnecessary; it also forbids cursing, swearing, blaspheming, and profane words.[59]

210. **What is an oath?**

An oath is the calling God to witness that what we affirm is true, or that we will do what we promise.

211. **Is it ever lawful to swear?**

It is never lawful to swear what is false; but it is lawful to swear what is true whenever God's honor, or the good or the necessary defense of ourselves, or of our neighbor, requires it.

212. **What do you mean by an unjust oath?**

An unjust oath is an oath injurious to God, to ourselves, or to our neighbor.

THE CROWNING WITH THORNS

[59] Cf. Mt 5:34; Jas 5:12

213. **Is a person obliged to keep an unjust oath?**

A person is not obliged to keep an unjust oath: he sinned in taking it—and would also sin in keeping it.

214. **Is a person obliged to keep a lawful oath?**

A person is obliged to keep a lawful oath: it would be perjury to break it.

215. **What is perjury?**

It is perjury to break a lawful oath, or to take a false one.

216. **Is perjury a great sin?**

Perjury is a most grievous sin.

217. **What is a vow?**

A vow is a solemn promise made to God.

218. **Say the third commandment.**

The third commandment is: Remember that thou keep holy the sabbath-day.

219. **What is commanded by the third commandment?**

We are commanded by the third commandment to sanctify the Sunday by prayer and other religious duties.

220. **Which is the chief duty of religion by which we are to sanctify the Sunday?**

The chief duty of religion, by which we should sanctify the Sunday, is the hearing of Mass devoutly.

221. **What other good works are particularly recommended to sanctify the Sunday?**

The other particular good works recommended to sanctify the Sunday are to attend vespers, or evening devotions; to read pious books; and to perform the works of mercy, spiritual and corporal: particularly to instruct the ignorant in the way of salvation, both by word and example.[60]

222. **What is forbidden by the third commandment?**
The third commandment forbids all unnecessary servile work on Sunday, and whatever may hinder the due observance of the Lord's day, or may tend to profane it.

223. **Say the fourth commandment.**
The fourth commandment is: Honor thy father and thy mother.

224. **What is commanded by the fourth commandment?**
We are commanded by the fourth commandment to love, honor, and obey our parents and superiors.[61]

225. **What is forbidden by the fourth commandment?**
The fourth commandment forbids all contempt, stubbornness, ill-will, and disobedience to parents and superiors.

226. **What are the chief duties of parents?**
The chief duties of parents are to provide for their children; to instruct them and all others under their care, in the Christian doctrine, and other knowledge necessary for them; and by every means in their power to lead them to God.[62]

227. **What special reward has God promised to dutiful children?**
The special reward promised by God to dutiful children is a long life and happiness, even in this world.[63]

---

[60] Cf. Dn 12:3
[61] Cf. Col 3:18-22
[62] Cf. 1 Tm 5:8
[63] Cf. Eph 6:1-3

228. **What are the duties of subjects to the temporal powers?**

The duties of subjects to the temporal powers are to be subject to them, and to honor and obey them, not only for wrath, but also for conscience sake; for so is the will of God.[64]

229. **Does the scripture require any other duty of subjects?**

The scripture also requires us to show respect to those who rule over us, to pray "for kings, and for all who are in high station, that we may lead a quiet and peaceable life."[65]

230. **What are the chief duties of masters to their servants, apprentices, and all others under their care?**

The chief duties of masters to their servants are: to lead them to God by word and example, to see that they be exact in their religious duties, to treat them with justice and humanity, and to correct and reprove them when necessary.

231. **What does St. Paul say to masters?**

St. Paul says: "Masters, do to your servants that which is just and equal, knowing that you also have a master in heaven."[66]

232. **What are the chief duties of servants and apprentices to their masters?**

The chief duties of servants and apprentices to their masters are: to be obedient, respectful, and faithful to them; to be diligent in their work and services; and not to suffer their masters to be injured in their property by any person.[67]

[64] Cf. 1 Pt 2:13ff; Rom 13:1-8
[65] 1 Tm 2:2
[66] Col 4:1
[67] Cf. Eph 6:5-8; Col 3:22-24

LESSON 18

On the Fifth, Sixth, Seventh, and Eighth Commandments

233. **Say the fifth commandment.**

The fifth commandment is: Thou shalt not kill.

234. **What is forbidden by the fifth commandment?**

The fifth commandment forbids all willful murder, quarrelling, fighting, drunkenness, hatred, anger, and revenge.

235. **What else is forbidden by the fifth commandment?**

The fifth commandment also forbids all injurious words, the giving of scandal or bad example, and not to ask pardon of those whom we have offended.[68]

236. **Say the sixth commandment.**

The sixth commandment is: Thou shalt not commit adultery.

237. **What is forbidden by the sixth commandment?**

The sixth commandment forbids all unchaste freedom with another's wife or husband.

238. **What else is forbidden by the sixth commandment?**

The sixth commandment also forbids all immodest actions, looks, or, words, all immodest songs, novels, and plays, and everything that is contrary to chastity.[69]

239. **Is it sinful to take part in such immodest practices?**

It is sinful to join in such immodest practices, to encourage them, or to be present at them.

---

[68] Cf. Mt 5:39
[69] Cf. Col 3:5

240. **Say the seventh commandment.**

The seventh commandment is: Thou shalt not steal.

241. **What is forbidden by the seventh commandment?**

The seventh commandment forbids all unjust taking or keeping what belongs to another.

242. **What else is forbidden by the seventh commandment?**

The seventh commandment also forbids all cheating in buying or selling, or any other injury done to our neighbor in his property.[70]

243. **What is commanded by the seventh commandment?**

We are commanded by the seventh commandment to pay our lawful debts, and to give everyone his own.

244. **What are they obliged to do who retain ill-gotten goods, or who keep unjustly what belongs to another?**

They who have ill-gotten goods or keep unjustly what belongs to another, must restore them as soon as possible, so far as they are able, otherwise the sin will not be forgiven them.

245. **Say the eighth commandment.**

The eighth commandment is: Thou shalt not bear false witness against thy neighbor.

246. **What is forbidden by the eighth commandment?**

The eighth commandment forbids all false testimonies, rash judgment, and lies.[71]

---

[70] Cf. 1 Cor 6:10
[71] Cf. Mt 7:1

247. **Is it lawful to tell an innocent or jocose lie, or to tell a lie for a good purpose?**
No lie can be lawful or innocent, and no motive, however good, can excuse a lie—because a lie is always sinful and bad in itself.[72]

248. **What else is forbidden by the eighth commandment?**
The eighth commandment also forbids all backbiting, calumny, detraction, and all words and speeches hurtful to our neighbor's honor or reputation.

249. **What is commanded by the eighth commandment?**
We are commanded by the eighth commandment to speak of others with justice and charity—as we would be glad they would speak of us—and to say nothing but the truth.

250. **What must they do who have given false evidence against a neighbor, or who have spoken ill of him, or injured his character in any respect?**
They who have injured their neighbor's character in any way must repair the injury as far as they are able and as soon as possible—otherwise the sin will not be forgiven them.

LESSON 19

On the Ninth and Tenth Commandments

251. **Say the ninth commandment.**
The ninth commandment is: Thou shalt not covet thy neighbor's wife.

252. **What is forbidden by the ninth commandment?**
The ninth commandment forbids all immodest thoughts and desires, and all willful pleasure in them.

---

[72] Cf. Jn 8:44

253. **What else is forbidden by the ninth commandment?**

The ninth commandment also forbids all immediate occasions of immodest thoughts and desires.

254. **What are the immediate occasions of immodest thoughts and desires?**

The immediate occasions of immodest thoughts and desires are: unchaste words and discourses, immodest books and pictures, and all amusements dangerous to chastity.

255. **What else may be deemed immediate occasions of immodest thoughts and desires?**

Improper looks, idleness, bad company, all excess in eating and drinking, and whatever tends to inflame the passions, may also be deemed immediate occasions of immodest thoughts and desires.

256. **Is it sinful to have unchaste thoughts, when there is no intention or desire to commit any criminal action?**

Unchaste thoughts are always very dangerous, and when they are entertained deliberately and with pleasure, they defile the soul like criminal actions.[73]

257. **Say the tenth commandment.**

The tenth commandment is: Thou shalt not covet thy neighbor's goods.

258. **What is forbidden by the tenth commandment?**

The tenth commandment forbids all covetous thoughts and desires of our neighbor's goods or profits.

259. **To how many commandments may the ten commandments be reduced?**

The ten commandments may be reduced to these two principal commandments, which are the two great precepts of charity: "Thou shalt love the Lord thy God with thy whole heart, and with thy whole soul, and with all

---

[73] Cf. Mt 5:28

JESUS CARRYING HIS CROSS

thy strength, and with all thy mind; and thy neighbor as thyself...this do, and thou shalt live."[74]

260. **"Who is my neighbor?"[75]**

My neighbor is all mankind of every description, without any exception of persons—even those who injure us, or differ from us in religion.

261. **How am I to love my neighbor as myself?**

"As you would," says Christ, "that men should do to you, do you also to them in like manner."[76]

[74] Lk 10:27-28
[75] Lk 10:29
[76] Lk 6:31

262. **What particular duties are required by that rule?**

We are required never to injure our neighbor by word or action, in his person, property, or character—always to wish well to him, and to pray for him—and to assist him, as far as we are able, in his spiritual and corporal necessities.

263. **Are we also obliged to love our enemies?**

Most certainly we are obliged to love our enemies. "Love your enemies," says Christ, "do good to them that hate you, bless them that curse you, and pray for them that persecute and calumniate you."[77]

Chapter 7

LESSON 20

On the Precepts of the Church

264. **Are there any other commandments besides the ten commandments of God?**

Besides the commandments of God there are the commandments or precepts of the Church, which are chiefly six.

265. **Say the six commandments of the Church.**

The commandments of the Church are:

1. To hear Mass on Sundays and all holy days of obligation.
2. To fast and abstain on the days commanded.
3. To confess our sins at least once a year.
4. To receive worthily the Blessed Eucharist at Easter, or within the time appointed: that is, from Ash Wednesday to Trinity Sunday.

[77] Lk 6:27-28; Mt 5:44

5. To contribute to the support of our pastors.
6. Not to solemnize marriage at the forbidden times, nor to marry persons within the forbidden degrees of kindred, nor otherwise prohibited by the Church, nor clandestinely.

266. **Is it a mortal sin not to hear Mass on a Sunday or holy day?**
It is a mortal sin not to hear Mass on a Sunday or holy day of obligation if the omission be culpable—and fathers and mothers, masters and mistresses, and all such persons, sin grievously, if, without sufficient cause, they hinder children, servants, or any others subject to them, from hearing Mass on a Sunday or such holy day.[78]

267. **What do you mean by holy days?**
Holy days are certain solemn days ordered by the Church to be kept holy.

268. **Why were holy days instituted by the Church?**
Holy days were instituted by the Church to recall to our minds, with praise and thanksgiving, the great mysteries of religion—and the virtues and rewards of the saints, and that we might glorify God on them.

269. **How are we to keep holy days?**
We are to keep the holy days as we should keep Sundays.

270. **What are we obliged to do by the second commandment of the Church?**
We are obliged by the second commandment of the Church to give part of the year to fast and abstinence.[79]

271. **What do you mean by fast days?**
Fast days are certain days on which we are allowed but one meal, and are forbidden flesh meat.

[78] Cf. 2 Thes 3:4
[79] Cf. Mt 6:16-18

272. **What do you mean by days of abstinence?**

Days of abstinence are certain days on which we are forbidden to eat flesh meat, but are allowed the usual number of meals.

273. **Why does the Church command us to fast and abstain?**

The Church commands us to fast and abstain in order that we may mortify our sinful passions and appetites, and satisfy for our sins by doing penance for them.

THE CRUCIFIXION

274. **Why does the Church command us to abstain from flesh meat on Fridays?**

The Church commands us to abstain from flesh meat on Fridays in honor and commemoration of our Savior's death.

LESSON 21

The Precepts of the Church Continued

275. **What means the commandment of confessing our sins at least once a year?**
The commandment of confessing our sins at least once a year means that we are obliged, under pain of mortal sin, to go to confession within the year, and we are threatened with severe penalties by the Church if we neglect doing so.

276. **Does a bad confession satisfy the obligation of confessing our sins once a year?**
A bad confession does not satisfy our obligation, but renders us more guilty, by the additional crime of sacrilege.

277. **Is it sufficient to go but once a year to confession?**
Frequent confession is necessary for all those who frequently fall into mortal sin or who are in the occasion of sin—and for all who desire to advance in virtue.

278. **At what age are children obliged to go to confession?**
Children are obliged to go to confession as soon as they are capable of committing sin—that is, when they come to the use of reason, which is generally supposed to be about the age of seven years.

279. **Where, and from whom are we to receive the Blessed Eucharist at Easter?**
We are to receive the Blessed Eucharist at Easter in our own parish and from our own pastor; or elsewhere, with his leave.

280. **At what age are children obliged to receive the Blessed Eucharist?**
Children are obliged to receive the Blessed Eucharist as soon as they are able to discern the body of the Lord—that is, when they understand what

the Blessed Eucharist is, and how they should be prepared to receive it worthily.[80]

281. **Are we obliged in conscience and justice, and by divine precept, to contribute to the support of our pastors?**

We are obliged in conscience and justice, and by divine precept, to contribute to the support of our pastors. St. Paul says: "So the Lord ordained that they who preach the gospel should live by the gospel."[81]

282. **Is a clandestine marriage a valid and a good marriage?**

Wherever the decree of the Council of Trent (which annuls clandestine marriages) has been duly published, a clandestine marriage is no marriage—it is null and void in the sight of God and of his Church.[82]

283. **What is a clandestine marriage?**

Every marriage of a Catholic is a clandestine marriage if the parish priest of the parish where the marriage is celebrated is not present, or another priest by his leave, or by leave of the bishop; together with at least two witnesses.

284. **Do the precepts of the Church oblige under pain of mortal sin?**

The precepts of the Church oblige under pain of mortal sin, "He that will not hear the church," says Christ, "let him be to thee as the heathen and the publican."[83]

285. **What is necessary to keep the commandments of God and of his Church?**

The grace of God, which is obtained chiefly by prayer and the sacraments, is necessary to keep the commandments of God and of his Church.

---

[80] Cf. 1 Cor 11:29
[81] 1 Cor 9:13-14
[82] Cf. Council of Trent, Session 24, Ch. 1
[83] Mt 18:17; Cf. Lk 10:16

Chapter 8

LESSON 22

On Prayer

286. **What is prayer?**

Prayer is an elevation of the soul to God, to adore him, to bless his holy name, to praise his goodness, and to return him thanks for his benefits.

287. **Is prayer anything else?**

Prayer is also a humble petition to God for all necessaries for soul and body.

288. **When should we pray?**

Christ himself says, "We ought always to pray."[84]

289. **How can we always pray?**

We can always pray by offering to God all our thoughts, words, and actions; by keeping ourselves in the state of grace; and by praying at certain times.

290. **At what particular times should we pray?**

We should pray particularly on Sundays and holy days; every morning and every night; and in all dangers, temptations, and afflictions.

291. **After what manner should we pray?**

We should pray with all possible attention and devotion—and in a respectful posture, on bended knees.

[84] Lk 18:1

292. **What conditions are necessary to render our prayers acceptable?**

We must always offer our prayers with a humble and contrite heart, with fervor and perseverance, with confidence in God's goodness, with resignation to his will, and in the name of Jesus Christ.

293. **What do you say of those who at their prayers think not of God, or of what they say?**

If our distractions at prayers be willful, our prayers, instead of pleasing God, offend him, and are an abomination to him.[85]

294. **What prayers are most recommended to us?**

The prayers most recommended to us are: the Lord's Prayer, the Hail Mary, the Apostles' Creed, and the *confiteor*, or general confession.

295. **Does the Church also recommend the acts of faith, hope, and charity?**

The Church recommends the acts of faith, hope, and charity; they are an excellent form of prayer, and remind us of our chief duties to God.

296. **What are our chief duties to God?**

Our chief duties to God are to believe in him, to hope in him, and to love him.

297. **Why do you make an act of contrition before the acts of faith, hope, and charity?**

We make an act of contrition before the other acts in order to obtain pardon of our sins—and thereby to render our prayers more acceptable to God, and more beneficial to ourselves.

[85] Cf. Mt 15:7-8

LESSON 23

On the Lord's Prayer and the Hail Mary

298. Who made the Lord's Prayer?

Our Lord Jesus Christ made the Lord's Prayer,[86] and it is therefore called the Lord's Prayer.

299. Whom do you call "Our Father" when you begin the Lord's Prayer?

"Our Father" is Almighty God, Father, Son, and Holy Ghost, who is the common Father of all.

300. What means, "Hallowed be thy name"?

By "Hallowed be thy name," we beg that God's name may be praised and glorified by all his creatures.

301. What means, "Thy kingdom come"?

By "Thy kingdom come," we beg that God may reign in our hearts by his grace in this life—and that we may reign forever with him in the next.

302. What means, "Thy will be done"?

By "Thy will be done," we beg that God would enable us, by his grace, to do his will in all things on earth, as the angels and saints do in heaven.

303. What means, "Give us this day our daily bread"?

By "Give us this day our daily bread," we beg for all necessaries for our souls and bodies.

304. What means, "Forgive us our trespasses as we forgive them who trespass against us"?

By "Forgive us our trespasses as we forgive them who trespass against us," we beg that God would forgive us our offenses, as we forgive them who offend us.

---

[86] Cf. Mt 6:9-13

305. **Will God forgive us our offenses, if we do not forgive our enemies and all those who have offended us?**

God will show no mercy to us, unless we forgive from our hearts our enemies, and all those who have offended or injured us.[87]

306. **What means, "Lead us not into temptation"?**

By "Lead us not into temptation," we beg that God would strengthen us against all temptations.

307. **What means, "Deliver us from evil"?**

By "Deliver us from evil," we beg that God would deliver us, in body and soul, from all evil, particularly that of sin.

308. **Who made the Hail Mary?**

The angel Gabriel and St. Elizabeth made the first part of the Hail Mary, and the Church made the last part.[88]

309. **Is it lawful to honor the Virgin Mary?**

It is lawful to honor the Blessed Virgin, since God himself so much honored her, and the scripture says, "all nations shall call (her) blessed."[89]

310. **What honor do we give our Blessed Lady?**

We honor our Blessed Lady more than all the other saints, because she is the Mother of God—but we never give her divine or supreme honor, which is due to God alone.

311. **Why do Catholics so often repeat the Hail Mary?**

Catholics often repeat the Hail Mary to honor the mystery of the incarnation, which that prayer expresses, and to show their great respect and devotion to the Mother of God—and their special confidence in her assistance, particularly at the hour of death.

[87] Cf. Mt 18:35; 6:15
[88] Cf. Lk 1:28, 42
[89] Lk 1:48

312. **And why do you say the Hail Mary after the Lord's Prayer?**

We say the Hail Mary after the Lord's Prayer that, by our Blessed Lady's intercession, we may more easily obtain what we ask for in the Lord's Prayer.

Chapter 9

LESSON 24

On the Sacraments in General, and on Baptism

313. **By what other means besides prayer can we obtain the grace of God?**

The sacraments are, together with prayer, the most powerful of all means for obtaining the grace of God.

314. **What is a sacrament?**

A sacrament is a visible, that is, an outward sign or action, instituted by Christ to give grace.

315. **Whence have the sacraments the power of giving grace?**

The sacraments have the power of giving grace from the merits of Christ, which they apply to our souls.

316. **Why are so many ceremonies used in the administration of the sacraments?**

Ceremonies are used in the administration of the sacraments to excite devotion and reverence to them and to signify and explain their effects.

317. **How many sacraments are there?**

There are seven sacraments: baptism, confirmation, Eucharist, penance, extreme unction, holy orders, and matrimony.

318. **What is baptism?**

Baptism is a sacrament which cleanses us from original sin, makes us Christians, children of God, and heirs to the kingdom of heaven.

319. **Does baptism also remit the actual sins committed before it?**

Baptism remits the actual sins committed before it, and all the punishments due to them.

320. **Is baptism necessary to salvation?**

Baptism is necessary to salvation, for without baptism we "cannot enter the kingdom of God."[90]

321. **Who are appointed by Christ to give baptism?**

The pastors of his Church are appointed to give baptism—but, in case of necessity, any layman or woman can give it.

322. **How is baptism given?**

Baptism is given by pouring water on the head of the person to be baptized, saying while pouring the water, "I baptize thee in the name of the Father, and of the Son, and of the Holy Ghost."[91]

323. **What do we promise in baptism?**

We promise in baptism to renounce the devil with all his works and pomps.

LESSON 25

On Confirmation

324. **What is confirmation?**

Confirmation is a sacrament which makes us strong and perfect Christians.

---

[90] Jn 3:5
[91] Cf. Mt 28:19

325. **How does the bishop give confirmation?**
The bishop gives confirmation by the imposition of hands, and by prayer—that is, he holds out his hands, and prays while doing so, that the Holy Ghost may descend upon those who are to be confirmed—and then he makes the sign of the cross on their foreheads with chrism.[92]

326. **Why does the bishop give those he confirms a stroke on the cheek?**
The bishop gives a stroke upon the cheek to put them in mind that by confirmation they are strengthened to suffer, and, if necessary, even to die for Christ.

327. **To receive confirmation worthily, is it necessary to be in a state of grace?**
To receive confirmation worthily, it is necessary to be in a state of grace: and children of an age to learn should be instructed in the Christian doctrine.

328. **What special preparation should be made for confirmation?**
The special preparation for confirmation is to make a good confession, and by fervent prayer to beseech your heavenly Father to send his Holy Spirit on you.[93]

329. **What do you think of those who receive confirmation in the state of mortal sin?**
They who receive confirmation in the state of mortal sin add to their former guilt the horrid crime of sacrilege.

330. **What graces are received by confirmation?**
The graces received in confirmation are the seven gifts of the Holy Ghost.

[92] Cf. Acts 8:14-17
[93] Cf. Lk 11:13

331. **Repeat the seven gifts of the Holy Ghost.**

The seven gifts of the Holy Ghost are: wisdom, understanding, counsel, fortitude, knowledge, piety, and the fear of the Lord.

332. **What obligations do we contract by confirmation?**

The obligations we contract by confirmation are to profess our faith openly; not to deny our religion on any occasion whatsoever; and, like good soldiers of Christ, to be faithful to him unto death.[94]

333. **Is it a great sin to neglect confirmation?**

It is a great sin to neglect confirmation, especially in those evil days, when faith and morals are exposed to so many and such violent temptations.

LESSON 26

On the Blessed Eucharist

334. **What is the Blessed Eucharist?**

The Blessed Eucharist is the sacrament of the body and blood, soul and divinity of Jesus Christ, under the appearances of bread and wine.

335. **What means the word *eucharist*?**

The word *eucharist* means a special grace or gift of God—and it also means a solemn act of thanksgiving to God for all his mercies.

336. **What do you mean by the appearances of bread and wine?**

By the appearances of bread and wine I mean the taste, color, and form of bread and wine, which still remain after the substance of the bread and wine has been changed into the body and blood of Christ.

[94] Cf. Apoc 2:10

337. **Are both the body and blood of Christ under the appearance of bread and under the appearance of wine?**
We believe that Christ, true God and true man, is whole and entire, under the appearance of either bread or wine.

338. **Are we to believe that the God of all glory is under the appearance of our corporal food?**
We believe that the God of all glory is under the appearance of our corporal food, just as we believe that the same God of all glory suffered death under the appearance of a criminal on the cross.

339. **How can the bread and wine become the body and blood of Christ?**
The bread and wine become the body and blood of Christ, by the goodness and power of God, with whom "no word shall be impossible."[95]

340. **Are we assured that Christ changed the substance of bread and wine into his body and blood?**
By the very words which Christ himself said when he instituted the Blessed Eucharist at his last supper, we know that he changed the substance of bread and wine into his body and blood.

341. **Which are the words Christ said when he instituted the Blessed Eucharist?**
When instituting the Blessed Eucharist, Christ said: "This is my body... this is my blood."[96]

342. **Did Christ give power to the priests of his Church to change bread and wine into his body and blood?**
Christ gave power to the priests of his Church to change bread and wine into his body and blood when he said to his apostles at his last supper, "Do this for a commemoration of me."[97]

---

[95] Lk 1:37
[96] Mt 26:26, 28
[97] Lk 22:19

343. **Why did Christ give to the priests of his Church so great a power?**

He gave to his priests this great power, that his children throughout all ages and nations might have a most acceptable sacrifice to offer to their heavenly Father—and that they might have this most precious food to nourish their souls.

344. **What is a sacrifice?**

A sacrifice is that first and most necessary act of religion, whereby we acknowledge God's supreme dominion over us, and our total dependence on him.

345. **What is the sacrifice of the new law?**

The Mass is the sacrifice of the new law.

346. **What is the Mass?**

The Mass is the sacrifice of the body and blood of Christ, which are really present under the appearances of bread and wine and offered to God, by the priest, for the living and the dead.

347. **Is the Mass a different sacrifice from that of the cross?**

The Mass is not a different sacrifice from that of the cross—it is the very same sacrifice, though offered in a different manner.

348. **Why do you say the Mass is the same sacrifice as that of the cross?**

The Mass is the same sacrifice as that of the cross, because in both we have the same victim and the same offerer; for the same Christ, who once offered himself a bleeding victim to his heavenly Father on the cross, continues to offer himself in an unbloody manner, by the hands of his priests on our altars.

349. **Was the Mass offered in the old law?**

The Mass was not offered in the old law. So great a sacrifice was reserved for the new law—which was to fulfill the figures of the old law, and to give to religion its full perfection.

350. **At what part of the Mass are the bread and wine changed into the body and blood of Christ?**

The bread and wine are changed into the body and blood of Christ at the consecration.

THE RESURRECTION

351. **By whom are the bread and wine changed into the body and blood of Christ?**

The bread and wine are changed into the body and blood of Christ by the priest—but it is by the power and words of Christ, whose Person the priest represents at the awful moment of consecration.

352. **What are the ends for which Mass is said?**

The ends for which Mass is said are: to give God honor and glory; to thank him for his benefits; to obtain remission of our sins, and all other graces and blessings, through Jesus Christ.

353. **For what other end is Mass offered?**

Another end for which Mass is offered is, to continue and represent the sacrifice of Christ on the cross till his second coming. "This do," says Christ, "in remembrance of me."[98]

354. **How should we assist at Mass?**

We should assist at Mass with great interior recollection and piety, and with every mark of outward respect and devotion.

355. **Which is the best manner of hearing Mass?**

The best manner of hearing Mass is, to offer it to God with the priest for the same purpose for which it is said, to meditate on Christ's sufferings, and to go to Communion.

LESSON 27

On Communion and Penance

356. **What do you mean by going to Communion?**

By going to Communion, I mean receiving the Blessed Eucharist.

357. **Is it advisable to go often to Communion?**

It is advisable to go often to Communion, as nothing can conduce more to a holy life. "He that eateth this bread," says Christ, "shall live forever."[99]

---

[98] 1 Cor 11:24
[99] Jn 6:59

358. How must we be prepared for Communion?

To be prepared for Communion we must be in the state of grace, and we must have a lively faith, a firm hope, and an ardent charity.[100]

359. What does it mean to be in the state of grace?

To be in the state of grace means to be free, at least, from the guilt of mortal sin.

360. How are we to have a lively faith?

We are to have a lively faith by firmly believing that in the Blessed Eucharist Jesus Christ himself—true God and true man—is really present with his very flesh and blood, his soul and divinity.

361. How are we to have a firm hope?

We are to have a firm hope by placing great confidence in the goodness of Christ, who gives himself to us in this banquet of love.

362. And how are we to have an ardent charity?

We are to have an ardent charity by returning love for love to Christ, and by devoting ourselves, in earnest, to his service all the days of our lives.

363. Is anything else required before Communion?

Yes; it is also required before Communion that we be fasting from midnight; and we should appear very modest and humble, and clean in dress—showing in our exterior the greatest devotion and reverence to so holy a sacrament.

364. What should we do after Communion?

After Communion we should spend some time in meditation and prayer—and particularly in acts of thanksgiving.

[100] Cf. 1 Cor 11:28

365. **Is it a great sin to receive unworthily?**

It is a great sin to receive unworthily, for whosoever receives unworthily is guilty of the body and blood of the Lord and eats judgment, that is, damnation to himself, not discerning the body of the Lord.[101]

366. **What do you mean by receiving unworthily?**

By receiving unworthily I mean receiving the Blessed Eucharist in the state of mortal sin.

367. **What should a person do if he be in mortal sin before Communion?**

He who is in mortal sin must obtain pardon in the sacrament of penance before he goes to Communion.

368. **What is penance?**

Penance is a sacrament by which the sins are forgiven which are committed after baptism.

369. **By whose power are sins forgiven?**

Sins are forgiven by the power of God, which Christ left to the pastors of his Church.

370. **When did Christ leave to the pastors of his Church the power of forgiving sins?**

Christ gave to the pastors of his Church the power of forgiving sins when he said to his apostles: "Receive ye the Holy Ghost. Whose sins you shall forgive, they are forgiven them; and whose sins you shall retain they are retained."[102]

371. **What must we do to obtain pardon of our sins in the sacrament of penance?**

To obtain pardon of our sins in the sacrament of penance we must make a good confession.

[101] Cf. 1 Cor 11:27-29
[102] Jn 20:22-23

LESSON 28

On Confession and on Indulgences

372. **What is confession?**
Confession is a sorrowful declaration of our sins made to a priest in order to obtain forgiveness.

373. **What is the best method to prepare for a good confession?**
The best method to prepare for a good confession is, first, earnestly to beg of God the grace to make a good confession; secondly, to examine carefully our conscience; thirdly, to make acts of faith, hope, and charity; and, fourthly, to excite ourselves to a sincere contrition for our sins.

374. **On what are we to examine our conscience?**
We are to examine our conscience on the commandments of God and of his Church, on the seven deadly sins, and particularly on our predominant passion and the duties of our station in life, that we may know in what we have sinned, and how often, in thought, word, deed, and omission.

375. **What is contrition?**
Contrition is a heartfelt sorrow and detestation of sin for having offended God, with a firm resolution of sinning no more.

376. **How may we excite ourselves to contrition?**
We may excite ourselves to contrition by the following motives: the fear of hell, the loss of heaven, the filthiness of sin, our ingratitude in offending God who is so good to us, and the injury our sins do to God, who is infinitely good in himself.

377. **Do you recommend any other motive to excite sorrow for our sins?**
Another motive to excite sorrow for our sins is to consider that the Son of God died for our sins, and that we crucify him again as often as we offend him.

378. **Which of these motives is the best to excite contrition?**

The best motive to excite contrition is, to be sorry for our sins because they offend God, who is infinitely good and perfect in himself.

379. **What must we do at confession?**

At confession we must beg the priest's blessing, say the *confiteor*, accuse ourselves of our sins, listen attentively to his instructions, and renew our sorrow when he gives absolution.

380. **What is absolution?**

Absolution is the sentence of pardon given by the priest, as minister of God in the sacrament of penance.

381. **What do you think of those who conceal a mortal sin in confession?**

Those who conceal a mortal sin in confession commit a most grievous sin by telling a lie to the Holy Ghost,[103] and, instead of obtaining pardon, they incur much more the wrath of God.

382. **What must persons do who did not carefully examine their consciences, or who had not sincere sorrow for their sins, or who willfully concealed a mortal sin in confession?**

Persons who did not examine their consciences, or who had not sorrow for their sins, or who willfully concealed a mortal sin in confession, must truly repent of all such bad and sacrilegious confessions, and must make them over again.

383. **What is the surest sign that our confessions were good, and that we had sincere sorrow for our sins?**

The surest sign that our confessions were good and that we had sincere sorrow for our sins is the amendment of our lives.

---

[103] Cf. Acts 5:1-5

384. What should we do after confession?

After confession we should give God thanks for having forgiven us our sins, and perform the penance enjoined by the confessor.

385. What do you mean by penance enjoined by the confessor?

By the penance enjoined by the confessor I mean the prayers and other good works which he enjoins on penitents, in satisfaction for their sins.

386. What is satisfaction?

Satisfaction is a reparation of the injury and insult offered to God by sin, and of the injustice done to our neighbor.

387. Will the penance enjoined in confession always satisfy for our sins?

The penance enjoined in confession will not always satisfy in full for our sins; but whatever else is wanting may be supplied by indulgences, and by our own penitential exercises.

388. What does the Church teach concerning indulgences?

The Church teaches that Christ gave power to the Church to grant indulgences, and that they are most useful to Christian people.[104]

389. What is meant by an indulgence?

By an indulgence is meant the remission, through the power of the Church, of the temporal punishment due to sin which sometimes remains after the sin itself is forgiven.

390. Has the Church power to grant indulgences?

The Church has power to grant indulgences: "Whatsoever," says Christ to St. Peter, "thou shalt loose upon earth, it shall be loosed also in heaven."[105]

---

[104] Cf. Council of Trent, Session 25, Ch. 21
[105] Mt 16:19; Cf. 2 Cor 2:10

391. **To whom does the Church grant indulgences?**

The Church grants indulgences to such only as are in the state of grace, and sincerely desirous to amend their lives, and to satisfy God's penitential works.

392. **Is an indulgence a pardon for sins to come or a license to commit sin?**

An indulgence is not a pardon for sins to come, nor a license to commit future sin. It cannot even remit past sins; for mortal sin must be remitted, and a person must be in the state of grace, before gaining an indulgence.

393. **Why does the Church grant indulgences?**

The Church grants indulgences to assist our weakness, and to supply our insufficiency in satisfying the divine justice for our transgressions.

394. **When the Church grants indulgences what does it offer to God to supply our weakness and insufficiency, and in satisfaction for our sins?**

The Church in granting indulgences offers to God the infinite and superabundant merits of Christ, together with the virtues and the good works of his Virgin Mother and of all his saints.

395. **What conditions are generally necessary to gain indulgences?**

The conditions generally necessary to gain indulgences are: a good confession and Communion, and a faithful compliance with the other good works, which the Church requires on such occasions.

396. **What are the other good works which the Church usually prescribes in order to gain indulgences?**

The other good works which the Church usually prescribes in order to gain indulgences are: prayer, fasting, and almsdeeds.

397. **Are prayer, fasting, and almsdeeds promoted by indulgences?**

Indulgences promote prayer, fasting, and almsdeeds, as well as confession and Communion—and on this account also they are most useful to Christian people.

LESSON 29

On Extreme Unction, Holy Orders, and Matrimony

398. What is extreme unction?

Extreme unction is a sacrament which gives grace to die well, and is instituted chiefly for the spiritual strength and comfort of dying persons.

399. Is extreme unction given to all persons in danger of death?

Extreme unction is given to such only as are in danger of death by sickness.

THE ASCENSION

400. How should we prepare ourselves for extreme unction?

We should be prepared for extreme unction by a good confession, and we
should be truly sorry for all our sins, and resigned to the will of God, when
we are receiving that last sacrament.

401. **Who are appointed to administer the sacrament of extreme unction?**

The priests of the Church are appointed to administer the sacrament of extreme unction, as St. James teaches[106]—and so the Church has constantly practiced.

402. **What is holy orders?**

Holy orders is a sacrament which gives bishops, priests, and inferior clergy to the Church, and enables them to perform their several duties.[107]

403. **What is matrimony?**

Matrimony is a sacrament which gives grace to the husband and wife to live happy together, and to bring up their children in the fear and love of God.[108]

404. **Do they receive the grace of the sacrament of matrimony who contract marriage in the state of mortal sin?**

They who contract marriage in the state of mortal sin are guilty of a sacrilege, by profaning so great a sacrament[109]—and, instead of a blessing, they receive their condemnation.

405. **What should persons do to receive worthily the sacrament of marriage?**

To receive worthily the sacrament of marriage, they should make a good confession, and earnestly beseech God to grant them a pure intention, and direct them in the choice they are making.

406. **Should children consult their parents on their intended marriages?**

According to reason and religion, children should consult their parents on their intended marriages, and be advised by them; they should also give timely notice to their pastor.

---

[106] Cf. Jas 5:14-15
[107] Cf. Phil 1:1
[108] Cf. Mt 19:6
[109] Cf. Eph 5:32

407. **Why do so many marriages prove unhappy?**

So many marriages prove unhappy, because many enter into that holy state from unworthy motives, and with guilty consciences; therefore their marriages are not blessed by God.

408. **Can the bond or tie of marriage be ever broken?**

The bond or tie of marriage cannot be broken, except by the death of the husband or of the wife.[110]

409. **Can the sacraments be received more than once?**

All the sacraments can be received more than once, except baptism, confirmation, and holy orders, which imprint on the soul a character or spiritual mark that can never be effaced.

410. **Which sacraments are most necessary to us?**

The sacraments most necessary to us are baptism and penance.

411. **Why did Christ institute the sacraments?**

Christ instituted the sacraments for the sanctification of our souls, and to prepare us for a happy and glorious resurrection.

[110] Cf. Mt 19:3-9; Rom 7:1-3; 1 Cor 7

Chapter 10

LESSON 30

On the General Judgment

412. **What means the resurrection of the body?**

The resurrection of the body means, that we shall all rise again on the last day with the same bodies which we had in this life.

413. **What do you mean by the last day?**

By the last day is meant the day of general judgment, when we must all appear before the judgment seat of Christ; and then he will render to everyone according to his works.[111]

414. **Will our bodies rise united to our souls?**

Our bodies will rise united to our souls, in order to share in the soul's eternal bliss or misery.

415. **How are the bodies of the saints to rise?**

The bodies of the saints are to rise glorious and immortal.[112]

416. **Are the bodies of the damned to rise glorious?**

The bodies of the damned shall not rise glorious, but shall be immortal, to live forever in eternal flames.[113]

---

[111] Cf. 2 Cor 5:10; Mt 16:27
[112] Cf. 1 Cor 15:42-45
[113] Cf. 1 Cor 15:51

417. **In what manner will Christ come to judge us?**

Christ will come to judge us in the clouds of heaven, with great power and majesty, and all the angels with him.[114]

418. **As everyone is judged immediately after death, what need is there of a general judgment?**

There is need of a general judgment, that the providence of God, which often, in this world, permits the good to suffer and the wicked to prosper appear just before all men.

419. **What will Christ say to the good on the last day?**

Christ will say to the good on the last day: "Come, ye blessed of my Father, possess the kingdom prepared for you."[115]

420. **What will Christ say to the wicked on the last day?**

Christ shall say to the wicked on the last day: "Depart from me, ye cursed, into everlasting fire, which was prepared for the devil and his angels."[116]

421. **Where shall the wicked go at the last day?**

The wicked shall go, both body and soul, "into everlasting punishment."[117]

422. **And where will the just go on the last day?**

The just will enter, with glorious and immortal bodies, "into life everlasting."[118]

423. **What means life everlasting?**

Life everlasting means, that if we serve God faithfully in this life, we will be happy with him forever in heaven.

---

[114] Cf. Mt 24:30-31
[115] Mt 25:34
[116] Mt 24:41
[117] Mt 25:46
[118] Ibid.

424. What is the happiness of heaven?

The happiness of heaven is to see, love, and enjoy God in the kingdom of his glory forever and ever. Amen.

425. What means Amen?

Amen means, so be it.

The Manner of Serving a Priest at Mass

P: *Introibo ad altare Dei.*

C: *Ad Deum qui laetificat juventutem meam.*

P: *Judica me Deus, et discerne causam meam de gente non sancta, ab homine iniquo et doloso erue me.*

C: *Quia tu es, Deus, fortitudo mea, quare me repulisti et quare tristis incedo dum affligit me inimicus.*

P: *Emitte lucem tuam et veritatem tuam: ipsa me deduxerunt et adduxerunt in montem sanctum tuum, et in tabernacula tua.*

C: *Et introibo ad altare Dei, ad Deum qui laetificat juventutem meam.*

P: *Confitebor tibi in cithara Deus, Deus meus: Quare tristis es anima mea, et quare conturbas me.*

C: *Spera in Deo, quoniam adhuc confitebor illi, salutare vultus mei et Deus meus.*

P: *Gloria Patri, et Filio, et Spiritui Sancto.*

C: *Sicut erat in principio, et nunc, et semper, et in saecula saeculorum. Amen.*

P: *Introibo ad altare Dei.*

C: *Ad Deum qui laetificat juventutem meam.*

P: *Adjutorium nostrum in nomine Domini.*

C: *Qui fecit coelum et terram.*

P: *Confiteor Deo, etc.*

C: *Misereatur tui omnipotens Deus, et dimissis peccatis tuis perducat te ad vitam aeternam.*

P: *Amen.*

C: *Confiteor Deo omnipotenti, Beatae Mariae semper Virgini, beato Michaeli archangelo, beato Joanni Baptistae, sanctis apostolis Petro et Paulo, omnibus sanctis, et tibi, Pater, quia peccavi nimis cogitatione, verbo et opere, mea culpa, mea culpa, mea maxima culpa. Ideo precor Beatam Mariam, semper Virginem, beatum Michaelem archangelum, beatum Joannem Baptistam, sanctos apostolos Petrum et Paulum, omnes sanctos, et te Pater, orare pro me ad Dominum Deum nostrum.*

P: *Misereatur vestri, etc.*

C: *Amen.*

P: *Indulgentiam, absolutionem, etc.*

C: *Amen.*

P: *Deus tu conversus vivificabis nos.*

C: *Et plebs tua laetabitur in te.*

P: *Ostende nobis Domine misericordiam tuam.*

C: *Et salutare tuum da nobis.*

P: *Domine, exaudi orationem meam.*

C: *Et clamor meus ad te veniat.*

P: *Dominus vobiscum.*

C: *Et cum spiritu tuo.*

P: *Kyrie eleison.*

C: *Kyrie eleison.*

P: *Kyrie eleison.*

C: *Christe eleison.*

P: *Christe eleison.*

C: *Christe eleison.*

P: *Kyrie eleison.*

C: *Kyrie eleison.*

P: *Kyrie eleison.*

P: *Dominus vobiscum, or flectamus genua.*

C: *Et cum spiritu tuo, or levate.*

P: *Per omnia saecula saeculorum.*

C: *Amen.*

At the end of the epistle say, *Deo gratias.*

P: *Sequentia sancti evangelii, etc.*

C: *Gloria tibi Domine.*

At the end of the gospel say, *Laus tibi Christe.*

P: *Dominus vobiscum.*

C: *Et cum spiritu tuo.*

P: *Orate fratres.*

C: *Suscipiat Dominus sacrificium de manibus tuis; ad laudem et gloriam nominis sui; ad utilitatem quoque nostram totiusque Ecclesiae suae sanctae.*

P: *Per omnia saecula saeculorum.*

C: *Amen.*

P: *Dominus vobiscum.*

C: *Et cum spiritu tuo.*

P: *Sursum corda.*

C: *Habemus ad Dominum.*

P: *Gratias agamus Domino Deo nostro.*

C: *Dignum et justum est.*

P: *Per omnia saecula saeculorum.*

C: *Amen.*

P: *Et ne nos inducas in tentationem.*

C: *Sed libera nos a malo.*

P: *Per omnia saecula saeculorum.*

C: *Amen.*

P: *Pax Domini sit semper vobiscum.*

C: *Et cum spiritu tuo.*

P: *Dominus vobiscum.*

C: *Et cum spiritu tuo.*

P: *Per omnia saecula saeculorum.*

C: *Amen.*

P: *Ite missa est, or benedicamus Domino.*

C: *Deo gratias.*

P: *Requiescant in pace.*

C: *Amen.*

DESCENT OF THE HOLY GHOST

Pro Fidelibus Defunctis

P: *De profundis clamavi ad te Domine; Domine, exaudi vocem meam.*

C: *Fiant aures tuae intendentes in vocem deprecationis meae.*

P: *Si iniquitates observaveris Domine, Domine, quis sustinebit.*

C: *Quia apud te propitiatio est: et propter legem tuam sustinui te Domine.*

P: *Sustinuit anima mea in verbo ejus; speravit anima mea in Domino.*

C: *A custodia matutina usque ad noctem speret Israel in Domino.*

P: *Quia apud Dominum misericordia, et copiosa apud eum Redemptio.*

C: *Et ipse redimet Israel ex omnibus iniquitatibus ejus.*

P: *Requiem aeternam dona eis Domine.*

C: *Et lux perpetua luceat eis.*

P: *A porta inferi.*

C: *Erue Domine animas eorum.*

P: *Requiescant in pace.*
C: *Amen.*
P: *Domine exaudi orationem meam.*
C: *Et clamor meus ad te veniat.*
P: *Dominus vobiscum.*
C: *Et cum spiritu tuo.*

Oremus.
Fidelium Deus omnium conditor et Redemptor animabus famulorum famularum-
que tuarum remissionem cunctorum tribue peccatorum ut indulgentiam quam sem-
per optaverunt piis supplicationibus consequantur. Qui vivis et regnas, etc.

Litany of Our Lord Jesus Christ

Lord, have mercy on us.
Christ, have mercy on us.
Lord, have mercy on us.
Christ, have mercy on us.
Jesus, hear us.
Jesus, graciously hear us.

God the Father of heaven, have mercy on us.
God the Son, Redeemer of the world, have mercy on us.
God the Holy Ghost, have mercy on us.
Holy Trinity, one God, have mercy on us.

Jesus, Son of the living God, have mercy on us.
Jesus, splendor of the Father, have mercy on us.
Jesus, brightness of eternal light, have mercy on us.
Jesus, king of glory, have mercy on us.
Jesus, sun of justice, have mercy on us.
Jesus, Son of the Virgin Mary, have mercy on us.
Jesus, most amiable, have mercy on us.

Jesus, most admirable, have mercy on us.
Jesus, mighty God, have mercy on us.
Jesus, father of the world to come, have mercy on us.
Jesus, angel of great counsel, have mercy on us.
Jesus, most powerful, have mercy on us.
Jesus, most patient, have mercy on us.
Jesus, most obedient, have mercy on us.
Jesus, meek and humble of heart, have mercy on us.
Jesus, lover of chastity, have mercy on us.
Jesus, lover of us, have mercy on us.
Jesus, God of peace, have mercy on us.
Jesus, author of life, have mercy on us.
Jesus, example of virtues, have mercy on us.
Jesus, zealous lover of souls, have mercy on us.
Jesus, our God, have mercy on us.
Jesus, our refuge, have mercy on us.
Jesus, father of the poor, have mercy on us.
Jesus, treasure of the faithful, have mercy on us.
Jesus, good shepherd, have mercy on us.
Jesus, true light, have mercy on us.
Jesus, eternal wisdom, have mercy on us.
Jesus, infinite goodness, have mercy on us.
Jesus, our way, and our life, have mercy on us.
Jesus, joy of angels, have mercy on us.
Jesus, king of patriarchs, have mercy on us.
Jesus, master of apostles, have mercy on us.
Jesus, teacher of evangelists, have mercy on us.
Jesus, strength of martyrs, have mercy on us.
Jesus, light of confessors, have mercy on us.
Jesus, purity of virgins, have mercy on us.
Jesus, crown of all saints, have mercy on us.

Be merciful unto us: spare us, O Jesus.
Be merciful unto us: hear us, O Jesus.

From all evil, Lord Jesus, deliver us.

From all sin, Lord Jesus, deliver us.

From thy wrath, Lord Jesus, deliver us.

From the snares of the devil, Lord Jesus, deliver us.

From the spirit of fornication, Lord Jesus, deliver us.

From everlasting death, Lord Jesus, deliver us.

From a neglect of thy holy inspirations, Lord Jesus, deliver us.

Through the mystery of thy holy incarnation, Lord Jesus, deliver us.

Through thy nativity, Lord Jesus, deliver us.

Through thine infancy, Lord Jesus, deliver us.

Through thy most divine life, Lord Jesus, deliver us.

Through thy labors, Lord Jesus, deliver us.

Through thine agony and passion, Lord Jesus, deliver us.

Through thy cross and dereliction, Lord Jesus, deliver us.

Through thy pains and torments, Lord Jesus, deliver us.

Through thy death and burial, Lord Jesus, deliver us.

Through thy resurrection, Lord Jesus, deliver us.

Through thine ascension, Lord Jesus, deliver us.

Through thy joys, Lord Jesus, deliver us.

Through thy glory, Lord Jesus, deliver us.

Lamb of God, who takest away the sins of the world: spare us, O Lord Jesus.

Lamb of God, who takest away the sins of the world: hear us, O Lord Jesus.

Lamb of God, who takest away the sins of the world: hear us, O Lord Jesus.

Christ Jesus, hear us.

Christ Jesus, graciously hear us.

V: May the name of the Lord be blessed.

R: From henceforth and forever.

Let us pray.

O Lord Jesus Christ, who hast said, "Ask, and you shall receive; seek, and you shall find; knock, and it shall be opened unto you," give, we beseech thee to us who ask, the grace of thy most divine love, that with all our hearts, words, and works, we may love thee, and never cease to praise thee. Who livest and reignest with the Father and the Holy Ghost, one God, world without end. Amen.

THE

SHORT CATECHISM

EXTRACTED FROM

THE CATECHISM

Ordered by the National Synod of Maynooth, and approved of by the Cardinal, the Archbishops, and Bishops of Ireland, for general use throughout the Irish Church.

Imprimatur:

✠ EDUARDUS CARD. MACCABE,
ARCHIEPISCOPUS DUBLINENSIS,
HIBERNIÆ PRIMAS.

Copyright.

DUBLIN:

M. H. GILL & SON, O'CONNELL STREET.

1891.

Original Title Page

THE

Short Catechism

EXTRACTED FROM

The Catechism

Ordered by the National Synod of Maynooth, and
approved of by the Cardinal, the Archbishops, and
Bishops of Ireland, for general use
throughout the Irish Church.

Imprimatur:

✠ EDUARDUS CARD. MACCABE,
ARCHIEPISCOPUS DUBLINENSIS,
HIBERNIAE PRIMAS.

Copyright.

DUBLIN:
M. H. GILL & SON, O'CONNELL STREET.
1891.

Introductory Prayers

In the name of the Father, and of the Son, and of the Holy Ghost.
Amen.

The Lord's Prayer

Our Father, who art in heaven, hallowed be thy name. Thy kingdom come; thy will be done on earth as it is in heaven. Give us this day our daily bread; and forgive us our trespasses, as we forgive them who trespass against us; and lead us not into temptation, but deliver us from evil. Amen.

The Angelical Salutation

Hail, Mary! full of grace, the Lord is with thee; blessed art thou among women, and blessed is the fruit of thy womb, Jesus. Holy Mary! Mother of God, pray for us, sinners, now, and at the hour of our death. Amen.

The Apostles' Creed

I believe in God, the Father Almighty, Creator of heaven and earth, and in Jesus Christ, his only Son, our Lord, who was conceived by the Holy Ghost, born of the Virgin Mary; suffered under Pontius Pilate; was crucified, dead, and buried; he descended into hell; the third day he rose again from the dead; he ascended into heaven, and sitteth at the right hand of God, the Father Almighty; from thence he shall come to judge the living and the dead. I believe in the Holy Ghost, the holy Catholic Church, the communion of saints, the forgiveness of sins, the resurrection of the body, life everlasting. Amen.

The Confiteor

I confess to Almighty God, to Blessed Mary ever Virgin, to blessed Michael the archangel, to blessed John the Baptist, to the holy apostles Peter and Paul, and to all the saints, that I have sinned exceedingly in thought, word, and deed, through my fault, through my fault, through my most grievous fault. Therefore I beseech the Blessed Mary ever Virgin, the blessed Michael the archangel, the blessed John the Baptist, the holy apostles Peter and Paul, and all the saints, to pray to the Lord our God for me.

May the Almighty God have mercy on me, forgive me my sins, and bring me to life everlasting. Amen.

May the Almighty and merciful Lord grant me pardon, absolution, and remission of my sins. Amen.

Indulgenced Prayers

Jesus, Mary, and Joseph, I offer you my heart and soul.

Jesus, Mary, and Joseph, assist me in my last agony.

Jesus, Mary, and Joseph, may I breathe forth my soul in peace with you. (300 days indulgence.)

Let us pray.

O God! who in thine ineffable providence didst vouchsafe to choose blessed Joseph to be the spouse of thy most holy Mother, grant, we beseech thee, that we may be made worthy to receive him for our intercessor in heaven, whom we venerate as our holy and most powerful protector, who livest and reignest, world without end. Amen.

Grace before Meals

Bless us, O Lord, and these thy gifts which of thy bounty we are about to receive, through Christ our Lord. Amen.

Grace after Meals

We give thee thanks, O Almighty God, for all thy benefits; who livest and reignest, world without end. Amen.

May the souls of the faithful departed, through the mercy of God, rest in peace. Amen.

Prayers to Be Said Previous to Teaching Catechism

In the name of the Father, and of the Son, and of the Holy Ghost. Amen.
Anthem: Come, O Holy Ghost, replenish the hearts of thy faithful, and enkindle in them the fire of thy love.
V: Send forth thy Spirit, and they shall be created.
R: And thou shall renew the face of the earth.
Prayer: O Lord God of infinite bounty and mercy, grant us, we beseech thee, the grace to be always directed and comforted by thy Holy Spirit through Jesus Christ. Amen.
Direct, we beseech thee, O Lord, our actions by thy inspirations, and carry them on by thy assistance; that every prayer, instruction, and other work of ours may begin always from thee, and by thee be happily ended, through Christ our Lord. Amen.

Prayer after Teaching Catechism

Grant us, we beseech thee, O Lord, the help of thy grace, that what by thy instructions we know is to be done, by thy assistance we may perfectly accomplish, through Jesus Christ our Lord. Amen.

Acts of Contrition, Faith, Hope, and Charity

Let us pray.

O Almighty and eternal God, grant unto us an increase of faith, hope, and charity; and that we may obtain what thou hast promised, make us to love and practice what thou commandest, through Jesus Christ our Lord. Amen.

An Act of Contrition

O my God! I am heartily sorry for having offended thee, and I detest my sins above every other evil, because they displease thee, my God, who for thy infinite goodness art so deserving of all my love; and I firmly resolve, by thy holy grace, never more to offend thee, and to amend my life.

Short Act of Contrition

O my God, I am heartily sorry for my sins, and I detest them because they offend thee, who art so good, and I firmly resolve, with the help of thy holy grace, never again to commit sin.

An Act of Faith

O my God! I firmly believe that thou art one only God, the Creator and sovereign Lord of heaven and earth, infinitely great and infinitely good. I firmly believe that in thee, one only God, there are three divine Persons, really distinct, and equal in all things— the Father, and the Son, and the Holy Ghost. I firmly believe that God the Son, the second Person of the most Holy Trinity, became man; that he was conceived by the Holy Ghost and was born of the Virgin Mary; that he suffered and died on a cross to redeem and save us; that he arose the third day from the dead; that he ascended into heaven; that he will come at the end of the world to judge mankind; that he will reward the good with eternal happiness, and condemn the wicked to the everlasting pains of hell. I believe these and all other articles which the holy Roman Catholic Church proposes to our belief, because thou, my God, the infallible truth, hast revealed them; and thou hast commanded us to hear the Church, which is the pillar and the ground of truth.[1] In this faith I am firmly resolved, by thy holy grace, to live and die.

An Act of Hope

O my God! who hast graciously promised every blessing, even heaven itself, through Jesus Christ, to those who keep thy commandments; relying on thy infinite power, goodness, and mercy, and on thy sacred promise, to which thou art always faithful, I confidently hope to obtain pardon of all my sins, grace to serve thee faithfully in this life, by doing the good works thou hast commanded, and which, with thy assistance, I now purpose to perform, and eternal happiness in the next, through my Lord and Savior Jesus Christ.

An Act of Charity

O my God! I love thee with my whole heart and soul, and above all things, because thou art infinitely good and perfect, and most worthy of all my love; and for thy sake, I love my neighbor as myself. Mercifully grant, O my God! that having loved thee on earth, I may love and enjoy thee forever in heaven. Amen.

[1] Cf. Mt 18:17; 1 Tm 3:15

The Angelus

1. The angel of the Lord declared unto Mary:
And she conceived of the Holy Ghost.
Hail Mary! full of grace, the Lord is with thee; blessed art thou among women, and blessed is the fruit of thy womb, Jesus. Holy Mary! Mother of God, pray for us, sinners, now, and at the hour of our death. Amen.
2. Behold the handmaid of the Lord:
Be it done unto me according to thy word.
Hail Mary and Holy Mary.
3. And the Word was made flesh:
And dwelt among us.
Hail Mary and Holy Mary.
Pray for us, O holy Mother of God.
That we may be made worthy of the promises of Christ.

Let us pray.
Pour forth, we beseech thee, O Lord, thy grace into our hearts, that we, to whom the incarnation of Christ, thy Son, was made known by the message of an angel, may, by his passion and cross, be brought to the glory of his resurrection, through the same Christ our Lord. Amen.

May the divine assistance always remain with us.
And may the souls of the faithful departed, through the mercy of God, rest in peace. Amen.

Chapter 1

LESSON 1

On God and the Creation of the World

1. **Who made the world?**

   God made the world.

2. **Who is God?**

   God is the Creator and sovereign Lord of heaven and earth and of all things.

3. **How many gods are there?**

   There is but one God, who will reward the good and punish the wicked.

4. **How many Persons are there in God?**

   In God there are three divine Persons, really distinct and equal in all things: the Father, the Son, and the Holy Ghost.

5. **Is the Father God?**

   The Father is God, and the first Person of the Blessed Trinity.

6. **Is the Son God?**

   The Son is God, and the second Person of the Blessed Trinity.

7. **Is the Holy Ghost God?**

   The Holy Ghost is God, and the third Person of the Blessed Trinity.

8. **What means the Blessed Trinity?**

   The Blessed Trinity means one God in three divine Persons.

9. **Are the three divine Persons three gods?**

   The three divine Persons are one only God, having but one and the same divine nature, and they are from eternity.

LESSON 2

On the Incarnation

10. **Did one of the divine Persons become man?**

    God the Son, the second divine Person, became man.

11. **How did God the Son become man?**

    God the Son became man by taking a body and soul like ours in the chaste womb of the Virgin Mary, by the power and operation of the Holy Ghost.

12. **How do you call God the Son made man?**

    God the Son made man is called Jesus Christ.

13. **What is the meaning of the words *Jesus Christ?***

    Jesus signifies *Savior*; and Christ signifies *the anointed*; and St. Paul says that "in the name of Jesus every knee should bend."[2]

14. **Did Jesus Christ remain God when he became man?**

    Jesus Christ remains always God.

15. **Was Jesus Christ always man?**

    Jesus Christ was man only from the time of his conception or incarnation.

16. **What means the incarnation?**

    The incarnation means, that God the Son, the second Person of the Blessed Trinity, was made man.

---

[2] Phil 2:10

17. **What do you believe Jesus Christ to be?**

    I believe Jesus Christ to be true God and true man.

18. **Why did God the Son become man?**

    God the Son became man to redeem and save us.

19. **How did Christ redeem and save us?**

    Christ redeemed and saved us by his sufferings and death on the cross.

20. **On what day did God the Son become man?**

    God the Son became man on the twenty-fifth of March, the day of the annunciation.

LESSON 3

On Jesus Christ

21. **On what day was Christ born of the Virgin Mary?**

    Christ was born on Christmas day, in a stable at Bethlehem.

22. **How long did Christ live on earth?**

    Christ lived on earth about thirty-three years, and led a most holy life in poverty and sufferings.

23. **Why did Christ live so long on earth?**

    Christ lived so long upon earth to show us the way to heaven by his instructions and example.

24. **How did Christ end his life?**

    On Good Friday, Christ was crucified on Mount Calvary, and died nailed to a cross.

25. **Who condemned Christ to so cruel a death?**
Pontius Pilate, the Roman governor, condemned Christ to death at the desire of the Jews.

26. **What lessons do we learn from the sufferings and death of Christ?**
From the sufferings and death of Christ we learn the enormity of sin, the hatred God bears to it, and the necessity of satisfying for it.

27. **Where did Christ's soul go after his death?**
After Christ's death his soul descended into hell.

28. **Did Christ's soul descend into the hell of the damned?**
The hell into which Christ's soul descended was not the hell of the damned, but a place or state of rest called limbo, where the souls of the saints who died before Christ were detained.

29. **Where was Christ's body while his soul was in limbo?**
When Christ's soul was in limbo his body was in the sepulcher or grave.

30. **On what day did Christ rise from the dead?**
On Easter Sunday, the third day after his death, Christ arose in body and soul glorious and immortal from the dead.

31. **How long did Christ stay on earth after his resurrection?**
Christ stayed on earth forty days after his resurrection, to show that he was truly risen from the dead, and to instruct his apostles.

32. **After Christ had remained forty days on earth, where did he go?**
After forty days, Christ, on Ascension day, ascended from Mount Olivet, with his body and soul, into heaven.

33. **Where is Christ in heaven?**
Christ sits at the right hand of God the Father Almighty, in heaven.

Chapter 2

LESSON 4

On the Holy Ghost, the Sign of the Cross, the Church

34. **Did Christ make any special promise to his apostles before he ascended into heaven?**

    Before he ascended into heaven, Christ promised to his apostles that he would send the Holy Ghost, the Spirit of truth, to teach them all things, and to abide with them forever.[3]

35. **Why did Christ send the Holy Ghost?**

    Christ sent the Holy Ghost to sanctify his Church, to comfort his apostles, and to enable them to preach his gospel, or the new law.

36. **How do you call the followers of the new law?**

    The followers of the new law are called Christians.

37. **How are we known to be Christians?**

    We are known to be Christians by being baptized, by professing the doctrine of Christ, and by the sign of the cross.

38. **How is the sign of the cross made?**

    The sign of the cross is made by putting the right hand to the forehead, then under the breast, then to the left and right shoulders, saying: "In the name of the Father, and of the Son, and of the Holy Ghost. Amen."

[3] Cf. Jn 14:16-17; 15:26; 16:13

39. **Why do we make the sign of the cross?**
    We make the sign of the cross to beg that Jesus Christ, by his cross and passion, may bless and protect us.

40. **Should we frequently make the sign of the cross?**
    We should frequently make the sign of the cross, particularly in all temptations and dangers, and before and after prayer, but we should always make it with great attention and devotion.

41. **Where are true Christians to be found?**
    True Christians are to be found only in the true Church.

42. **How do you call the true Church?**
    The true Church is called the holy Catholic Church.

43. **Is there any other true Church besides the holy Catholic Church?**
    As there is but "one Lord, one faith, one baptism, one God and Father of all," there can be but the one true Church.[4]

44. **Are all obliged to be of the true Church?**
    All are obliged to belong to the true Church, and no one can be saved out of it.

45. **What other advantages have we in the true Church?**
    In the true Church, besides the true faith, we have the communion of saints and the forgiveness of sins.

46. **What means the forgiveness of sins?**
    The forgiveness of sins means, that Christ left to the pastors of his Church the power of forgiving sins.

[4] Eph 4:5-6

LESSON 5

On Sin and Purgatory

47. **What is sin?**

    Sin is any willful thought, word, deed, or omission contrary to the law of God.

48. **What is original sin?**

    Original sin is the sin we inherit from our first parents, and in which we were conceived and born "children of wrath."[5]

49. **Who were our first parents?**

    Our first parents were Adam and Eve, the first man and woman.

50. **What is mortal sin?**

    Mortal sin is a grievous offense or transgression against the law of God.

51. **Why is it called mortal?**

    Mortal sin is so called, because it kills the soul by depriving it of its true life, which is sanctifying grace, and because it brings everlasting death and damnation to the soul.

52. **What is venial sin?**

    Venial sin is a less grievous offense or transgression against the law of God.

53. **Does venial sin deprive the soul of sanctifying grace, and deserve everlasting punishment?**

    Venial sin does not deprive the soul of sanctifying grace, or deserve everlasting punishment, but it hurts the soul by lessening its love for God, and

---

[5] Eph 2:3

disposing it to mortal sin. The scripture says, "He that contemneth small things shall fall by little and little."[6]

54. **Is it a great misfortune to fall into mortal sin?**

To fall into mortal sin is the greatest of all misfortunes.

55. **Where do they go who die in mortal sin?**

They who die in mortal sin go to hell, for all eternity.

56. **What is hell?**

Hell is the place of eternal torments.

57. **Where do they go who have not done penance for their venial sins?**

They who die without doing penance for their venial sins go to purgatory.

58. **What is purgatory?**

Purgatory is a place or state of punishment in the next life where some souls suffer for a time before they go to heaven.

59. **Can the souls in purgatory be relieved by our prayers and other good works?**

As the souls in purgatory are children of God, and still members of the Church, they share in the communion of saints, and are relieved by our prayers and other good works: for the scripture says, "It is a holy and a wholesome thought to pray for the dead, that they may be loosed from their sins."[7]

60. **What does the communion of saints mean?**

The communion of saints is the union that exists between the members of the true Church on earth with each other, and with the blessed in heaven, and the suffering souls in purgatory.

[6] Ecclus 19:1
[7] 2 Mc 12:46

61. **What benefits follow from the communion of saints?**

Through the communion of saints the faithful on earth assist each other by their prayers and good works, and are aided by the intercession of the saints in heaven; whilst both the saints in heaven and the faithful on earth help the souls in purgatory.

62. **Is it sufficient for salvation to be members of the true Church?**

It is not sufficient for salvation to be members of the true Church; we must avoid evil and do good.[8]

63. **"What good shall I do that I may have life everlasting?"[9]**

"If thou wilt enter into life," says Christ, "keep the commandments."[10]

64. **What commandments am I to keep?**

I am to keep the ten commandments of God.

LESSON 6

On the Commandments of God and the Church

65. **Say the ten commandments of God.**

The ten commandments of God are:

1. I am the Lord thy God; thou shalt not have strange gods before me.
2. Thou shalt not take the name of the Lord thy God in vain.
3. Remember that thou keep holy the sabbath-day.
4. Honor thy father and thy mother.
5. Thou shalt not kill.
6. Thou shalt not commit adultery.
7. Thou shalt not steal.
8. Thou shalt not bear false witness against thy neighbor.

---

[8] Cf. Ps 33:15; Ps 36:27; 1 Pt 3:11
[9] Mt 19:16
[10] Mt 19:17

9. Thou shalt not covet thy neighbor's wife.

10. Thou shalt not covet thy neighbor's goods.

66. Is it necessary to keep all and every one of the ten commandments?

It is necessary to keep every one of the ten commandments; for the scripture says, whosoever shall offend in one, shall become guilty of all.[11]

67. What is an oath?

An oath is the calling God to witness that what we affirm is true, or that we will do what we promise.

68. What is perjury?

It is perjury to break a lawful oath, or to take a false one.

69. Is perjury a great sin?

Perjury is a most grievous sin.

70. To how many commandments may the ten commandments be reduced?

The ten commandments may be reduced to these two principal commandments, which are the two great precepts of charity: "Thou shalt love the Lord thy God with thy whole heart, and with thy whole soul, and with all thy strength, and with all thy mind, and thy neighbor as thyself...This do, and thou shalt live."[12]

71. Who is my neighbor?

My neighbor is all mankind of every description, without any exception of persons—even those who injure us, or differ from us in religion.

72. Are we also obliged to love our enemies?

Most certainly we are obliged to love our enemies. "Love your enemies,"

[11] Cf. Jas 2:10
[12] Lk 10:27-28

says Christ, "do good to them that hate you, bless them that curse you, and pray for them that persecute and calumniate you."[13]

73. **Are there any other commandments besides the ten commandments of God?**

Besides the commandments of God there are the commandments or precepts of the Church, which are chiefly six.

74. **Say the six commandments of the Church.**

The commandments of the Church are:

1. To hear Mass on Sundays and all holy days of obligation.
2. To fast and abstain on the days commanded.
3. To confess our sins at least once a year.
4. To receive worthily the Blessed Eucharist at Easter, or within the time appointed; that is, from Ash Wednesday to Ascension Thursday, or, where it is so permitted, to the octave day of SS. Peter and Paul.
5. To contribute to the support of our pastors.
6. Not to solemnize marriage at the forbidden times, nor to marry persons within the forbidden degrees of kindred, nor otherwise prohibited by the Church, nor clandestinely.

75. **Do the precepts of the Church oblige under pain of mortal sin?**

The precepts of the Church oblige under pain of mortal sin. "He that will not hear the church," says Christ, "let him be to thee as the heathen and the publican."[14]

76. **What is necessary to keep the commandments of God and of his Church?**

The grace of God, which is obtained chiefly by prayer and the sacraments, is necessary to keep the commandments of God and of his Church.

---

[13] Lk 6:27-28
[14] Mt 18:17

Chapter 3

LESSON 7

On Prayer and the Sacraments

77. **What is prayer?**

Prayer is an elevation of the soul to God, to adore him, to bless his holy name, to praise his goodness, and to return him thanks for his benefits.

78. **Is prayer anything else?**

Prayer is also a humble petition to God for all necessaries for soul and body.

79. **After what manner should we pray?**

We should pray with all possible attention, and devotion—and in a respectful posture on bended knees.

80. **At what particular times should we pray?**

We should pray particularly on Sundays and holy days, every morning and every night, and in all dangers, temptations, and afflictions.

81. **What conditions are necessary to render our prayers acceptable?**

We must always offer our prayers with a humble and contrite heart, with fervor and perseverance, with confidence in God's goodness, with resignation to his will, and in the name of Jesus Christ.

82. **What prayers are most recommended to us?**

The prayers most recommended to us are: the Lord's Prayer, the Hail Mary, the Apostles' Creed, and the *confiteor*, or general confession.

83. **Does the Church also recommend the acts of faith, hope, and charity?**

The Church recommends the acts of faith, hope, and charity; they are an excellent form of prayer, and remind us of our chief duties to God.

84. **What are our chief duties to God?**

Our chief duties to God are to believe in him, to hope in him, and to love him.

85. **By what other means besides prayer can we obtain the grace of God?**

The sacraments are, together with prayer, the most powerful of all means for obtaining the grace of God.

86. **What is a sacrament?**

A sacrament is a visible, that is, an outward sign or action, instituted by Christ to give grace.

87. **Whence have the sacraments the power of giving grace?**

The sacraments have the power of giving grace from the merits of Christ which they apply to our souls.

88. **How many sacraments are there?**

There are seven sacraments: baptism, confirmation, Eucharist, penance, extreme unction, holy orders, and matrimony.

LESSON 8

On Baptism, Confirmation, and the Blessed Eucharist

89. **What is baptism?**

Baptism is a sacrament which cleanses us from original sin; makes us Christians; children of God, and heirs to the kingdom of heaven.

90. **Is baptism necessary to salvation?**

Baptism is necessary to salvation; for without baptism, we "cannot enter into the kingdom of God."[15]

91. **Who are appointed by Christ to give baptism?**

The pastors of his Church are appointed to give baptism—but in case of necessity, any layman or woman can give it.

92. **How is baptism given?**

Baptism is given by pouring water on the head of the person to be baptized, saying while pouring the water, "I baptize thee in the name of the Father, and of the Son, and of the Holy Ghost."

93. **What do we promise in baptism?**

We promise in baptism to renounce the devil with all his works and pomps.

94. **What is confirmation?**

Confirmation is a sacrament which makes us strong and perfect Christians.

95. **What special preparation should be made for confirmation?**

The special preparation for confirmation is to make a good confession, and by fervent prayer to beseech your heavenly Father to send his Holy Spirit on you.

96. **What do you think of those who receive confirmation in the state of mortal sin?**

They who receive confirmation in the state of mortal sin add to their former guilt the horrid crime of sacrilege.

97. **What graces are received by confirmation?**

The graces received in confirmation are the seven gifts of the Holy Ghost.

[15] Jn 3:5

98. **Repeat the seven gifts of the Holy Ghost.**

The seven gifts of the Holy Ghost are: wisdom, understanding, counsel, fortitude, knowledge, piety, and the fear of the Lord.

99. **What obligations do we contract by confirmation?**

The obligations we contract by confirmation are to profess our faith openly; not to deny our religion on any occasion whatsoever; and, like good soldiers of Christ, to be faithful to him unto death.[16]

100. **Is it a great sin to neglect confirmation?**

It is a great sin to neglect confirmation, especially in those evil days, when faith and morals are exposed to so many and such violent temptations.

101. **What is the Blessed Eucharist?**

The Blessed Eucharist is the sacrament of the body and blood, soul and divinity of Jesus Christ, under the appearances of bread and wine.

102. **How can the bread and wine become the body and blood of Christ?**

The bread and wine become the body and blood of Christ, by the goodness and power of God, with whom "no word shall be impossible."[17]

LESSON 9

On Mass and Communion

103. **What is the Mass?**

The Mass is the sacrifice of the body and blood of Christ, which are really present under the appearances of bread and wine, and are offered to God, by the priest, for the living and the dead.

[16] Cf. Apoc 2:10
[17] Lk 1:37

104. What is a sacrifice?

A sacrifice is that first and most necessary act of religion, whereby we acknowledge God's supreme dominion over us, and our total dependence on him.

105. What are the ends for which Mass is said?

The ends for which Mass is said are: to give God honor and glory; to thank him for his benefits; to obtain remission of our sins, and all other graces and blessings, through Jesus Christ.

106. For what other end is Mass offered?

Another end for which Mass is offered is to continue and represent the sacrifice of Christ on the cross till his second coming. "This do," says Christ, "in remembrance of me."[18]

107. How should we assist at Mass?

We should assist at Mass with great interior recollection and piety—and with every mark of outward respect and devotion.

108. Which is the best manner of hearing Mass?

The best manner of hearing Mass is, to offer it to God with the priest for the same purpose for which it is said, to meditate on Christ's sufferings, and to go to Communion.

109. How must we be prepared for Communion?

To be prepared for Communion we must be in the state of grace, and we must have a lively faith, a firm hope, and an ardent charity.

110. What does it mean to be in the state of grace?

To be in the state of grace means to be free, at least, from the guilt of mortal sin.

[18] Lk 22:19; 1 Cor 11:24

111. **Is anything else required before Communion?**

Yes; it is also required before Communion that we be fasting from midnight; and we should appear very modest and humble, and clean in dress—showing in our exterior the greatest devotion and reverence to so holy a sacrament.

112. **What should we do after Communion?**

After Communion we should spend some time in meditation and prayer—and particularly in acts of thanksgiving.

113. **Is it a great sin to receive unworthily?**

It is a great sin to receive unworthily, for whosoever receives unworthily is guilty of the body and blood of the Lord, and eats judgment, that is, damnation to himself, not discerning the body of the Lord.[19]

114. **What do you mean by receiving unworthily?**

By receiving unworthily I mean receiving the Blessed Eucharist in the state of mortal sin.

115. **What should a person do if he be in mortal sin before Communion?**

He who is in mortal sin, must obtain pardon in the sacrament of penance before he goes to Communion.

LESSON 10

On Penance and Confession

116. **What is penance?**

Penance is a sacrament by which the sins are forgiven which are committed after baptism.

---

[19] Cf. 1 Cor 11:27-29

117. **What must we do to obtain pardon of our sins in the sacrament of penance?**
To obtain pardon of our sins in the sacrament of penance we must make a good confession.

118. **What is confession?**
Confession is a sorrowful declaration of our sins made to a priest in order to obtain forgiveness.

119. **What is the best method to prepare for a good confession?**
The best method to prepare for a good confession is, first, earnestly to beg of God the grace to make a good confession; secondly, to examine carefully our conscience; thirdly, to make acts of faith, hope, and charity; and, fourthly, to excite ourselves to a sincere contrition for our sins.

120. **On what are we to examine our conscience?**
We are to examine our conscience on the commandments of God and of his Church, on the seven deadly sins, and particularly on our predominate passion and the duties of our station in life, that we may know in what we have sinned, and how often, in thought, word, deed, and omission.

121. **What is contrition?**
Contrition is a heartfelt sorrow and detestation of sin for having offended God, with a firm resolution of sinning no more.

122. **What must we do at confession?**
At confession we must beg the priest's blessing, say the *confiteor*, accuse ourselves of our sins, listen attentively to his instructions, and renew our sorrow when he gives absolution.

123. **What is absolution?**
Absolution is the sentence of pardon given by the priest, as minister of God, in the sacrament of penance.

124. **What do you think of those who conceal a mortal sin in confession?**

Those who conceal a mortal sin in confession commit a most grievous sin by telling a lie to the Holy Ghost,[20] and, instead of obtaining pardon, they incur much more the wrath of God.

125. **What must persons do who did not carefully examine their consciences, or who had not sincere sorrow for their sins, or who willfully concealed a mortal sin in confession?**

Persons who did not examine their conscience, or who had not sorrow for their sins, or who willfully concealed a mortal sin in confession, must truly repent of all such bad and sacrilegious confessions, and must make them over again.

126. **What is the surest sign that our confessions were good, and that we had sincere sorrow for our sins?**

The surest sign that our confessions were good, and that we had sincere sorrow for our sins, is the amendment of our lives.

127. **What should we do after confession?**

After confession we should give God thanks for having forgiven us our sins, and perform the penance enjoined by the confessor.

128. **What do you mean by the penance enjoined by the confessor?**

By the penance enjoined by the confessor I mean the prayers and other good works which he enjoins on penitents, in satisfaction for their sins.

129. **Will the penance enjoined in confession always satisfy for our sins?**

The penance enjoined in confession will not always satisfy in full for our sins; but whatever else is wanting may be supplied by indulgences, and by our own penitential exercises.

[20] Cf. Acts 5:1-5

130. **What is meant by an indulgence?**

By an indulgence is meant the remission, through the power of the Church, of the temporal punishment due to sin, which sometimes remains after the sin itself is forgiven.

LESSON 11

On the Other Sacraments

131. **What is extreme unction?**

Extreme unction is a sacrament which gives grace to die well—and is instituted chiefly for the spiritual strength and comfort of dying persons.

132. **Is extreme unction given to all persons in danger of death?**

Extreme unction is given to such only as are in danger of death by sickness.

133. **How should we prepare ourselves for extreme unction?**

We should be prepared for extreme unction by a good confession, and we should be truly sorry for all our sins, and resigned to the will of God, when we are receiving that last sacrament.

134. **Who are appointed to administer the sacrament of extreme unction?**

The priests of the Church are appointed to administer the sacrament of extreme unction, as St. James teaches[21]—and so the Church has constantly practiced.

135. **What is holy orders?**

Holy orders is a sacrament which gives bishops, priests, and inferior clergy to the Church; and enables them to perform their several duties.

---

[21] Cf. Jas 5:14-15

136. **What is matrimony?**

Matrimony is a sacrament which gives grace to the husband and wife to live happy together, and to bring up their children in the fear and love of God.

137. **Do they receive the grace of the sacrament of matrimony who contract marriage in the state of mortal sin?**

They who contract marriage in a state of mortal sin are guilty of a sacrilege, by profaning so great a sacrament—and, instead of a blessing, they receive their condemnation.

138. **What should persons do to receive worthily the sacrament of marriage?**

To receive worthily the sacrament of marriage, they should make a good confession, and earnestly beseech God to grant them a pure intention, and direct them in the choice they are making.

139. **Why do so many marriages prove unhappy?**

So many marriages prove unhappy, because many enter into that holy state from unworthy motives and with guilty consciences; therefore their marriages are not blessed by God.

140. **Can the bond or tie of marriage be ever broken?**

The bond or tie of marriage cannot be broken, except by the death of the husband or of the wife.

141. **Can the sacraments be received more than once?**

All the sacraments can be received more than once, except baptism, confirmation, and holy orders, which imprint on the soul a character or spiritual mark that can never be effaced.

142. **Which sacraments are most necessary to us?**

The sacraments most necessary to us are baptism and penance.

143. **Why did Christ institute the sacraments?**

Christ instituted the sacraments for the sanctification of our souls—and to prepare us for a happy and glorious resurrection.

Chapter 4

LESSON 12

On the General Judgment

144. **What means the resurrection of the body?**

The resurrection of the body means, that we shall all rise again on the last day with the same bodies which we had in this life.

145. **What do you mean by the last day?**

By the last day is meant the day of general judgment, when we must all appear before the judgment seat of Christ; and then he will render to everyone according to his works.[22]

146. **Will our bodies rise united to our souls?**

Our bodies will rise united to our souls, in order to share in the soul's eternal bliss or misery.

147. **How are the bodies of the saints to rise?**

The bodies of the saints are to rise glorious and immortal.

148. **Are the bodies of the damned to rise glorious?**

The bodies of the damned shall not rise glorious, but shall be immortal, to live forever in eternal flames.

[22] Cf. 2 Cor 5:10; Mt 16:27; Rom 2:6

149. **In what manner will Christ come to judge us?**

Christ will come to judge us in the clouds of heaven, with great power and majesty and all the angels with him.[23]

150. **What will Christ say to the good on the last day?**

Christ will say to the good on the last day: "Come, ye blessed of my Father, possess the kingdom prepared for you."[24]

151. **What shall Christ say to the wicked on the last day?**

Christ shall say to the wicked on the last day: "Depart from me, ye cursed, into everlasting fire, which was prepared for the devil and his angels."[25]

152. **Where shall the wicked go at the last day?**

The wicked shall go, both body and soul, "into everlasting punishment."[26]

153. **And where will the just go on the last day?**

The just will enter, with glorious and immortal bodies, "into life everlasting."[27]

154. **What means life everlasting?**

Life everlasting means, that if we serve God faithfully in this life, we will be happy with him forever in heaven.

155. **What is the happiness of heaven?**

The happiness of heaven is to see, love, and enjoy God in the kingdom of his glory, forever and ever.

156. **What means Amen?**

Amen means, so be it.

---

23 Cf. Mt 24:30-31; 25:31; Lk 21:27
24 Mt 25:34
25 Mt 25:41
26 Mt 25:46
27 Ibid.

The Manner of Serving a Priest at Mass

P: *Introibo ad altare Dei.*

C: *Ad Deum qui laetificat juventutem meam.*

P: *Judica me Deus, et discerne causam meam de gente non sancta, ab homine iniquo et doloso erue me.*

C: *Quia tu es, Deus, fortitudo mea, quare me repulisti et quare tristis incedo dum affligit me inimicus.*

P: *Emitte lucem tuam et veritatem tuam: ipsa me deduxerunt et adduxerunt in montem sanctum tuum, et in tabernacula tua.*

C: *Et introibo ad altare Dei, ad Deum qui laetificat juventutem meam.*

P: *Confitebor tibi in cithara Deus, Deus meus: Quare tristis es anima mea, et quare conturbas me.*

C: *Spera in Deo, quoniam adhuc confitebor illi, salutare vultus mei et Deus meus.*

P: *Gloria Patri, et Filio, et Spiritui Sancto.*

C: *Sicut erat in principio, et nunc, et semper, et in saecula saeculorum. Amen.*

P: *Introibo ad altare Dei.*

C: *Ad Deum qui laetificat juventutem meam.*

P: *Adjutorium nostrum in nomine Domini.*

C: *Qui fecit coelum et terram.*

P: *Confiteor Deo, etc.*

C: *Misereatur tui omnipotens Deus, et dimissis peccatis tuis perducat te ad vitam aeternam.*

P: *Amen.*

C: *Confiteor Deo omnipotenti, Beatae Mariae semper Virgini, beato Michaeli archangelo, beato Joanni Baptistae, sanctis apostolis Petro et Paulo, omnibus sanctis, et tibi, Pater, quia peccavi nimis cogitatione, verbo et opere, mea culpa, mea culpa, mea maxima culpa. Ideo precor Beatam Mariam, semper Virginem, beatum Michaelem archangelum, beatum Joannem Baptistam, sanctos apostolos Petrum et Paulum, omnes sanctos, et te Pater, orare pro me ad Dominum Deum nostrum.*

P: *Misereatur vestri, etc.*

C: *Amen.*

P: *Indulgentiam, absolutionem, etc.*

C: *Amen.*

P: *Deus tu conversus vivificabis nos.*

C: *Et plebs tua laetabitur in te.*

P: *Ostende nobis Domine misericordiam tuam.*

C: *Et salutare tuum da nobis.*

P: *Domine, exaudi orationem meam.*

C: *Et clamor meus ad te veniat.*

P: *Dominus vobiscum.*

C: *Et cum spiritu tuo.*

P: *Kyrie eleison.*

C: *Kyrie eleison.*

P: *Kyrie eleison.*

C: *Christe eleison.*

P: *Christe eleison.*

C: *Christe eleison.*

P: *Kyrie eleison.*

C: *Kyrie eleison.*

P: *Kyrie eleison.*

P: *Dominus vobiscum, or flectamus genua.*

C: *Et cum spiritu tuo, or levate.*

P: *Per omnia saecula saeculorum.*

C: *Amen.*

At the end of the epistle say, *Deo gratias.*

P: *Sequentia sancti evangelii, etc.*

C: *Gloria tibi Domine.*

At the end of the gospel say, *Laus tibi Christe.*

P: *Dominus vobiscum.*

C: *Et cum spiritu tuo.*

P: *Orate fratres.*

C: *Suscipiat Dominus sacrificium de manibus tuis; ad laudem et gloriam nominis sui; ad utilitatem quoque nostram totiusque Ecclesiae suae sanctae.*

P: *Per omnia saecula saeculorum.*

C: *Amen.*

P: *Dominus vobiscum.*

C: *Et cum spiritu tuo.*

P: *Sursum corda.*

C: *Habemus ad Dominum.*

P: *Gratias agamus Domino Deo nostro.*

C: *Dignum et justum est.*

P: *Per omnia saecula saeculorum.*

C: *Amen.*

P: *Et ne nos inducas in tentationem.*

C: *Sed libera nos a malo.*

P: *Per omnia saecula saeculorum.*

C: *Amen.*

P: *Pax Domini sit semper vobiscum.*

C: *Et cum spiritu tuo.*

P: *Dominus vobiscum.*

C: *Et cum spiritu tuo.*

P: *Per omnia saecula saeculorum.*

C: *Amen.*

P: *Ite missa est, or benedicamus Domino.*

C: *Deo gratias.*

P: *Requiescant in pace.*

C: *Amen.*

Pro Fidelibus Defunctis

P: *De profundis clamavi ad te Domine; Domine, exaudi vocem meam.*

C: *Fiant aures tuae intendentes in vocem deprecationis meae.*

P: *Si iniquitates observaveris Domine, Domine, quis sustinebit.*

C: *Quia apud te propitiatio est: et propter legem tuam sustinui te Domine.*

P: *Sustinuit anima mea in verbo ejus; speravit anima mea in Domino.*

C: *A custodia matutina usque ad noctem speret Israel in Domino.*

P: *Quia apud Dominum misericordia, et copiosa apud eum Redemptio.*

C: *Et ipse redimet Israel ex omnibus iniquitatibus ejus.*

P: *Requiem aeternam dona eis Domine.*

C: *Et lux perpetua luceat eis.*

P: *A porta inferi.*

C: *Erue Domine animas eorum.*

P: *Requiescant in pace.*

C: *Amen.*

P: *Domine exaudi orationem meam.*

C: *Et clamor meus ad te veniat.*

P: *Dominus vobiscum.*

C: *Et cum spiritu tuo.*

Oremus.

Fidelium Deus omnium conditor et Redemptor animabus famulorum famularum-que tuarum remissionem cunctorum tribue peccatorum ut indulgentiam quam semper optaverunt piis supplicationibus consequantur. Qui vivis et regnas, etc.

Hymns

Jesus, the Very Thought of Thee

Jesus, the very thought of thee,
With sweetness fills my breast,
But sweeter far thy face to see,
And in thy presence rest.

Nor voice can sing, nor heart can frame,
Nor can the mem'ry find,

A sweeter sound than thy blest name,
O Savior of mankind.

O hope of every contrite heart,
O joy of all the meek;
To those who fall how kind thou art,
How good to those who seek.

But what to those who find? Ah this;
Nor tongue nor pen can show
The love of Jesus, what it is
None but his loved ones know.

O Jesus, love unchangeable,
For whom my soul doth pine;
O fruit of life celestial,
O sweetness all divine!

'Tis meet that I my love should give
Save thee to none beside;
And, dying to myself, should live
For Jesus crucified.

O Jesus! Jesus! Dearest Lord

O Jesus! Jesus! dearest Lord,
Forgive me if I say,
For very love, thy sacred name,
A thousand times a day.
A thousand times a day.

Oh, wonderful, that thou shouldst let
So vile a heart as mine,

Love thee with such a love as this
And make so free with thine.

O light in darkness, joy in grief,
O heaven begun on earth,
Jesus my love, my treasure,
Who can tell what thou art worth?

For thou to me art all in all,
My honor and my wealth
My heart's desire, my body's strength,
My soul's eternal health.

I'll Sing a Hymn to Mary

I'll sing a hymn to Mary,
The Mother of my God,
The Virgin of all virgins,
Of David's royal blood.
Oh! teach me, holy Mary,
A loving song to frame,
When wicked men blaspheme thee,
To love and bless thy name.

O lily of the valley,
O mystic rose, what tree
Or flower, e'en the fairest,
Is half so fair as thee?
Oh! let me, though so lowly,
Recite my Mother's fame,
When wicked men blaspheme thee,
I'll love and bless thy name.

O noble tower of David,
Of gold and ivory,
The ark of God's own promise,
The gate of heaven to me:
To live, and not to love thee,
Would fill my soul with shame;
When wicked men blaspheme thee,
I'll love and bless thy name.

When troubles dark afflict me,
In sorrow and in care,
Thy light doth ever guide me,
O beauteous morning star.
So I'll be ever ready,
Thy goodly help to claim,
When wicked men blaspheme thee,
To love and bless thy name.

The saints are high in glory,
With golden crowns so bright,
But brighter far is Mary,
Upon her throne of light:
Oh! that which God did give thee,
Let mortal ne'er disclaim;
When wicked men blaspheme thee,
I'll love and bless thy name.

But in the crown of Mary
There lies a wondrous gem,
As Queen of all the angels,
Which Mary shares with them,
"No sin hath e'er defiled thee,"
So doth our faith proclaim;
When wicked men blaspheme thee,

I'll love and bless thy name.

And now, O Virgin Mary,
My Mother and my Queen,
I've sung thy praise—so bless me
And keep my heart from sin;
When others jeer and mock thee
I'll often think how I,
To shield my Mother Mary,
Would lay me down and die.

Hail! Holy Joseph

Hail! holy Joseph, hail!
Chaste spouse of Mary, hail!
Pure as the lily flower,
In Eden's peaceful vale.

Hail! holy Joseph, hail!
Father of Christ esteem'd!
Father be thou to those
Thy foster Son redeem'd!

Hail! holy Joseph, hail!
Prince of the house of God!
May his best graces be
By thy sweet hands bestow'd.

Hail! holy Joseph, hail!
Belov'd of angels, hail!
Cheer thou the hearts that faint,
And guide the steps that fail.

Hail! holy Joseph, hail!
God's choice wert thou alone,
To thee the Word made flesh
Was subject as a Son.

Hail! holy Joseph, hail!
Teach us our flesh to tame;
And, Mary, keep the hearts
That love thy husband's name.

Mother of Jesus! bless,
And bless, ye saints on high,
All meek and simple souls
That to St. Joseph cry.

Kind Angel Guardian

Kind angel guardian, thanks to thee
For thy so watchful care of me.
Oh, lead me still, in ways of truth,
Dear guide of childhood and of youth.

Kind angel guardian, let my tears
Implore thee, too, for riper years;
Oh, keep me safe in wisdom's way,
And bring me back if I should stray.

When angry passions fill my soul,
Subdue them to thy meek control;
Through good and ill, oh, ever be
A guide, a guard, a friend to me.

And when death's hand shall seal mine eyes

Oh, bear my spirit to the skies,
And teach me there my voice to raise
In hymns of never-ending praise.

Litany of the Blessed Virgin Mary

Sub tuum praesidium confugimus, sancta Dei Genitrix, nostras deprecationes de despicias in necessitatibus nostris; sed a periculis cunctis libera nos semper, Virgo gloriosa, et benedicta.

We fly to thy patronage, O holy Mother of God! Despise not our prayers in our necessities, but deliver us from all dangers, O ever glorious and blessed Virgin.

Kyrie eleison.
Christe eleison.
Kyrie eleison.
Christe audi nos.
Christe exaudi nos.

Lord, have mercy on us.
Christ, have mercy on us.
Lord, have mercy on us.
Christ, hear us.
Christ, graciously hear us.

Pater de coelis, miserere nobis.

God, the Father of heaven, have mercy on us.

Fili Redemptor mundi Deus, miserere nobis.
Spiritus Sancte Deus, miserere nobis.

God, the Son, Redeemer of the world, have mercy on us.
God, the Holy Ghost, have mercy on us.

Sancta Trinitas, unus Deus, miserere nobis.

Holy Trinity, one God, have mercy on us.

Sancta Maria, ora pro nobis.
Sancta Dei Genitrix, ora pro nobis.
Sancta Virgo virginum, ora pro nobis.
Mater Christi, ora pro nobis.
Mater divinae gratiae, ora pro nobis.

Holy Mary, pray for us.
Holy Mother of God, pray for us.
Holy Virgin of virgins, pray for us.
Mother of Christ, pray for us.
Mother of divine grace, pray for us.

Mater purissima, ora pro nobis.
Mother most pure, pray for us.

Mater castissima, ora pro nobis.
Mother most chaste, pray for us.

Mater inviolata, ora pro nobis.
Mother undefiled, pray for us.

Mater intemerata, ora pro nobis.
Mother inviolate, pray for us.

Mater amabilis, ora pro nobis.
Mother most amiable, pray for us.

Mater admirabilis, ora pro nobis.
Mother most admirable, pray for us.

Mater Creatoris, ora pro nobis.
Mother of our Creator, pray for us.

Mater Salvatoris, ora pro nobis.
Mother of our Redeemer, pray for us.

Virgo prudentissima, ora pro nobis.
Virgin most prudent, pray for us.

Virgo veneranda, ora pro nobis.
Virgin most venerable, pray for us.

Virgo praedicanda, ora pro nobis.
Virgin most renowned, pray for us.

Virgo potens, ora pro nobis.
Virgin most powerful, pray for us.

Virgo clemens, ora pro nobis.
Virgin most merciful, pray for us.

Virgo fidelis, ora pro nobis.
Virgin most faithful, pray for us.

Speculum justitiae, ora pro nobis.
Mirror of justice, pray for us.

Sedes sapientiae, ora pro nobis.
Seat of wisdom, pray for us.

Causa nostrae laetitiae, ora pro nobis.
Cause of our joy, pray for us.

Vas spirituale, ora pro nobis.
Spiritual vessel, pray for us.

Vas honorabile, ora pro nobis.
Vessel of honor, pray for us.

Vas insigne devotionis, ora pro nobis.
Singular vessel of devotion, pray for us.

Rosa mystica, ora pro nobis.
Mystical rose, pray for us.

Turris Davidica, ora pro nobis.
Tower of David, pray for us.

Turris eburnea, ora pro nobis.
Tower of ivory, pray for us.

Domus aurea, ora pro nobis.
House of gold, pray for us.

Foederis arca, ora pro nobis.
Ark of the covenant, pray for us.

Janua coelis, ora pro nobis.
Gate of heaven, pray for us.

Stella matutina, ora pro nobis.
Morning star, pray for us.

Salus infirmorum, ora pro nobis.
Health of the sick, pray for us.

Refugium peccatorum, ora pro nobis.
Refuge of sinners, pray for us.

Consolatrix afflictorum, ora pro nobis.
Comforter of the afflicted, pray for us.

Auxilium Christianorum, ora pro nobis.
Help of Christians, pray for us.

Regina angelorum, ora pro nobis.
Queen of angels, pray for us.

Regina patriarcharum, ora pro nobis. Queen of patriarchs, pray for us.

Regina prophetarum, ora pro nobis. Queen of prophets, pray for us.

Regina apostolorum, ora pro nobis. Queen of apostles, pray for us.

Regina martyrum, ora pro nobis. Queen of martyrs, pray for us.

Regina confessorum, ora pro nobis. Queen of confessors, pray for us.

Regina virginum, ora pro nobis. Queen of virgins, pray for us.

Regina sanctorum omnium, ora pro nobis. Queen of all saints, pray for us.

Regina sine labe originali concepta, ora pro nobis. Queen conceived without original sin, pray for us.

Regina sanctissimi rosarii, ora pro nobis. Queen of the most holy rosary, pray for us.

Agnus Dei, qui tollis peccata mundi, parce nobis, Domine. Lamb of God, who takest away the sins of the world: spare us, O Lord.

Agnus Dei, qui tollis peccata mundi, exaudi nos, Domine. Lamb of God, who takest away the sins of the world: graciously hear us O Lord.

Agnus Dei, qui tollis peccata mundi, miserere nobis. Lamb of God, who takest away the sins of the world: have mercy on us.

Christe audi nos. Christ, hear us.

Christe exaudi nos. Christ, graciously hear us.

Kyrie eleison. Lord, have mercy on us.

Christe eleison. Christ, have mercy on us.

Kyrie eleison. Lord have mercy on us.

Pater noster, etc. Our Father, etc.

V: *Ora pro nobis, sancta Dei Genitrix.* **V:** Pray for us, O holy Mother of God.

R: *Ut digni efficiamur promissionibus Christi.* **R:** That we may be made worthy of the promises of Christ.

Oremus. Let us pray.

Concede nos famulos tuos, quaesumus, Domine Deus, perpetua mentis et corporis sanitate gaudere; et gloriosa Pour forth, we beseech thee, O Lord, thy grace into our hearts, that we to whom the incarnation

Beatae Mariae semper Virginis inter-
cessione, a praesenti liberari tristitia, et
aeterna perfrui laetitia, per Christum
Dominum nostrum. Amen.

of Christ thy Son was made
known by the message of an angel,
may, by his passion and cross, be
brought to the glory of his resurrection; through the same Christ
our Lord. Amen.

ABOUT THIS SERIES

Tradivox was first conceived as an international research endeavor to recover lost and otherwise little-known Catholic catechetical texts. As the research progressed over several years, the vision began to grow, along with the number of project contributors and a general desire to share these works with a broader audience.

Legally incorporated in 2019, Tradivox has begun the work of carefully remastering and republishing dozens of these catechisms which were once in common and official use in the Church around the world. That effort is embodied in this *Tradivox Catholic Catechism Index*, a multi-volume series restoring artifacts of traditional faith and praxis for a contemporary readership. More about this series and the work of Tradivox can be learned at www.Tradivox.com.

SOPHIA INSTITUTE

Sophia Institute is a nonprofit institution that seeks to nurture the spiritual, moral, and cultural life of souls and to spread the Gospel of Christ in conformity with the authentic teachings of the Roman Catholic Church.

Sophia Institute Press fulfills this mission by offering translations, reprints, and new publications that afford readers a rich source of the enduring wisdom of mankind.

Sophia Institute also operates the popular online resource CatholicExchange.com. *Catholic Exchange* provides world news from a Catholic perspective as well as daily devotionals and articles that will help readers to grow in holiness and live a life consistent with the teachings of the Church.

In 2013, Sophia Institute launched Sophia Institute for Teachers to renew and rebuild Catholic culture through service to Catholic education. With the goal of nurturing the spiritual, moral, and cultural life of souls, and an abiding respect for the role and work of teachers, we strive to provide materials and programs that are at once enlightening to the mind and ennobling to the heart; faithful and complete, as well as useful and practical.

Sophia Institute gratefully recognizes the Solidarity Association for preserving and encouraging the growth of our apostolate over the course of many years. Without their generous and timely support, this book would not be in your hands.

www.SophiaInstitute.com
www.CatholicExchange.com
www.SophiaInstituteforTeachers.org

Sophia Institute Press® is a registered trademark of Sophia Institute. Sophia Institute is a tax-exempt institution as defined by the Internal Revenue Code, Section 501(c)(3). Tax ID 22-2548708.